Jesus and His Jewish Influences

Jodi Magness, Ph.D.

PUBLISHED BY:

THE GREAT COURSES
Corporate Headquarters
4840 Westfields Boulevard, Suite 500
Chantilly, Virginia 20151-2299
Phone: 1-800-832-2412
Fax: 703-378-3819
www.thegreatcourses.com

Copyright © The Teaching Company, 2015

Printed in the United States of America

This book is in copyright. All rights reserved.

Without limiting the rights under copyright reserved above,
no part of this publication may be reproduced, stored in
or introduced into a retrieval system, or transmitted,
in any form, or by any means (electronic, mechanical,
photocopying, recording, or otherwise),
without the prior written permission of
The Teaching Company.

Jodi Magness, Ph.D.

Kenan Distinguished Professor
for Teaching Excellence in Early Judaism
The University of North Carolina
at Chapel Hill

Dr. Jodi Magness holds a senior endowed chair in the Department of Religious Studies at The University of North Carolina at Chapel Hill: the Kenan Distinguished Professor for Teaching Excellence in Early Judaism. Dr. Magness received her B.A. in Archaeology and History from The Hebrew University of Jerusalem in 1977 and her Ph.D. in Classical Archaeology from the University of Pennsylvania in 1989. From 1990 to 1992, she was a Mellon Postdoctoral Fellow in Syro-Palestinian archaeology at the Center for Old World Archaeology and Art at Brown University. From 1992 to 2002, she was Associate/Assistant Professor of Classical and Near Eastern Archaeology in the Departments of Classics and Art History at Tufts University.

Dr. Magness's most recent books are *The 2003–2007 Excavations in the Late Roman Fort at Yotvata* (coauthored with G. Davies); *The Archaeology of the Holy Land: From the Destruction of Solomon's Temple to the Muslim Conquest*; and *Stone and Dung, Oil and Spit: Jewish Daily Life in the Time of Jesus*. Her book *The Archaeology of Qumran and the Dead Sea Scrolls* won the Biblical Archaeology Society's Award for Best Popular Book on Archaeology for 2001–2002 and was selected as an Outstanding Academic Title for 2003 by *Choice: Current Reviews for Academic Libraries*. In addition, her book *The Archaeology of the Early Islamic Settlement in Palestine* was awarded the 2006 Irene Levi-Sala Book Prize for contributions in the archaeology of Israel in the nonfiction category.

Dr. Magness also has published dozens of articles in journals and edited volumes. Her research interests—which focus on Palestine in the Roman, Byzantine, and early Islamic periods and Diaspora Judaism in the Roman world—include ancient pottery, ancient synagogues, Qumran and the Dead Sea Scrolls, and the Roman army in the east.

Dr. Magness has participated in 20 excavations in Israel and Greece, including codirecting the 1995 excavations in the Roman siege works at Masada. From 2003 to 2007, she codirected excavations in the late Roman fort at Yotvata in Israel. Since 2011, she has directed excavations at Huqoq in Galilee (www.huqoq.org). Dr. Magness also consulted for and is featured in a National Geographic giant-screen film on Jerusalem, which was released in September 2013 and is showing around the world (www.jerusalemthemovie.com). In addition, for The Great Courses, she taught *The Holy Land Revealed*.

Dr. Magness's awards include a National Endowment for the Humanities Fellowship for college teachers and a Skirball Visiting Fellowship at the Oxford Centre for Hebrew and Jewish Studies (2000–2001); a Fulbright lecturing award at the Institute of Archaeology at The Hebrew University of Jerusalem (spring 2005); a fellowship at the School of Historical Studies at the Institute for Advanced Study in Princeton, NJ (2007–2008); and a Chapman Family Faculty Fellowship at the Institute for the Arts and Humanities at The University of North Carolina at Chapel Hill (2010–2011). In 2008, Dr. Magness received a national teaching honor: the Excellence in Undergraduate Teaching Award, given by the Archaeological Institute of America (AIA).

In January 2014, Dr. Magness was elected first vice president of the AIA. After serving a three-year term, she will become the next president of the AIA for another three-year term. Dr. Magness is also a member of the Managing Committee of the American School of Classical Studies at Athens. She has been a member (and past vice president) of the board of trustees of the W. F. Albright Institute of Archaeological Research in Jerusalem, the governing board of the AIA, and the board of trustees of The American Schools of Oriental Research. She also served as president of the North Carolina Society of the AIA and the Boston Society of the AIA. ■

Table of Contents

INTRODUCTION
Professor Biography i
Course Scope 1

LECTURE GUIDES

LECTURE 1
Jesus and Judaism 3

LECTURE 2
Sacred Mountains and Law Giving in Judaism 9

LECTURE 3
The United and Divided Israelite Kingdoms 15

LECTURE 4
The Destruction of Solomon's Temple 21

LECTURE 5
The Jewish and Samaritan Schism 27

LECTURE 6
The Jewish Diaspora and the Golden Rule 34

LECTURE 7
Alexander the Great's Impact on the Jews 41

LECTURE 8
Jews and Greek Rule: The Heliodorus Affair 48

LECTURE 9
Desolating Sacrilege and the Maccabean Revolt 54

LECTURE 10
Apocalyptic Works and the "Son of Man" 60

LECTURE 11
Jesus's Jewish Lineage 67

LECTURE 12
Was Jesus a Pharisee? 74

LECTURE 13
Jewish Ritual Purity: The Sons of Light 81

LECTURE 14
The Dead Sea Scrolls: Earliest Hebrew Bible 87

LECTURE 15
Was Jesus an Essene? 94

LECTURE 16
The Hebrew Scriptures and the Septuagint 101

LECTURE 17
The Reign of Herod the Great 107

LECTURE 18
Pontius Pilate: A Roman Prefect 114

LECTURE 19
Anarchy in Judea 121

LECTURE 20
Jesus's Prophecy: Jerusalem's Destruction 127

LECTURE 21
Flavius Josephus: Witness to 1st Century A.D. 134

LECTURE 22
Rabbinic Judaism's Traditions about Jesus 141

LECTURE 23
Jesus's Apocalyptic Outlook 148

LECTURE 24
Jesus's Teachings and Sayings in Context 155

SUPPLEMENTAL MATERIAL
Bibliography 161
Image Credits 164

Jesus and His Jewish Influences

Scope:

What did it mean to be a Jew in the late Second Temple period (2nd century B.C.–1st century A.D.)? Jesus was a product of the Judaism of his time—that is, early Judaism. Today, Jews gather in congregational buildings (synagogues), typically led by ordained rabbis, to worship the God of Israel through the reading of the Torah (Pentateuch = five books of Moses) and prayer. In contrast, in the time of Jesus, Jews worshipped the God of Israel in his house (the Jerusalem Temple), by gathering around an altar outside the temple, where priestly intermediaries offered sacrifices on their behalf.

In this course, we trace the origins of Judaism from the arrival of the Israelites in Canaan (c. 1200 B.C.) to the rise of Rabbinic Judaism (2nd–3rd centuries A.D.). We focus especially on the late Second Temple period, an era that witnessed a series of turbulent events: the temporary rededication of the Jerusalem Temple to Olympian Zeus and the outlawing of Judaism, which led to the outbreak of the Maccabean Revolt; the establishment of an independent Jewish kingdom under the Hasmoneans and the annexation of the Hasmonean kingdom to Rome; the reign of Herod the Great, a cruel man who ruled Judea as client king on behalf of Rome from 40 to 4 B.C.; the division of Herod's kingdom after his death, followed by increasing Jewish discontent under Roman maladministration, including that of the prefect Pontius Pilate; and the outbreak of a Jewish revolt 70 years after Herod's death, which culminated disastrously with the destruction of the Second Temple.

It was against the backdrop of this turmoil that different Jewish sects and movements emerged, including the Pharisees, Sadducees, and Essenes and Jesus's movement. All these groups were Jewish and observed biblical law, but they disagreed on the interpretation and practice of specific points of law, especially relating to ritual purity observance and the sacrificial cult in the Jerusalem Temple. The views of the Essenes and Jesus's movement were also influenced by apocalyptic expectations and an eschatological outlook, according to which they believed that the end of days was already underway. At the same time, the Gospel accounts indicate that Jesus's beliefs and practices differed in important ways from those of other groups, including the Pharisees and Essenes.

For information, we draw on various sources, including the Hebrew Bible, parabiblical and extrabiblical literature, the Dead Sea Scrolls, the writings of Philo of Alexandria and Flavius Josephus, the New Testament, and rabbinic literature. We consider the origins of early Judaism—the religion of the returning Babylonian exiles—including Ezra's implementation of a new prohibition against intermarriage and its effect on the Yahwistic population of Samaria (the Samaritans). We examine the impact on the Jews of Alexander the Great's conquest of the Near East in light of the spread of Greek culture in the centuries afterward. In addition, we discuss the flourishing Jewish Diaspora communities throughout the Near East, especially in Egypt. We consider different characteristics of Judaism in the time of Jesus, including the spread of apocalyptic expectations and the importance of biblical purity laws. The aim of this course is to provide an understanding of how Jesus's teachings and views were shaped by his Jewish background and context, illustrated by selected passages from the canonical Gospel accounts. The course ends with the rise of Rabbinic Judaism after the two Jewish revolts, a period that witnessed "the parting of the ways." ■

Lecture

1 Jesus and Judaism

This course will help you to understand Jesus's life and teachings within the context of early Judaism. Drawing on selected passages from the Old Testament and the New Testament, the course also sheds light on what the teachings and sayings attributed to Jesus meant to him and his first followers. The purpose of this lecture series is not to authenticate the Gospel accounts of Jesus's sayings and activities; rather, we will illustrate how the Gospel accounts fit within the context of early Judaism—that is, Judaism in the time of Jesus—and how the Gospels inform us about Jesus's life and ministry.

Defining Terms

- Today, the terms *Jew* and *Jewish* refer to people of a certain religion. Originally, however, these terms referred to someone of Judean origin—someone whose family came from the district of Judah, which was the geographical area centering on the city of Jerusalem. An important question is how the terms came to refer to people of a certain religion.

- In antiquity, every city or kingdom had its own special patron deity, even if the people of that city or kingdom worshipped many different gods. A noted example is the Greeks' Athena, the patron goddess of Athens. Although the people of Athens worshipped many different gods, Athena was their special patron deity; in fact, Athens was named after her.

- Similarly, the God of Israel was the patron deity of the Israelite tribes. Later, the God of Israel was the patron deity of the kingdoms of Israel and Judah. Therefore, in antiquity, a Jew was defined as someone from the geographical region of Judah, who worshipped the God of Israel—a definition that combined both geography and religion.

- The Greek term *Ioudaioi*, referring to the ancient Jews or Judeans, does not make a distinction between the religion and the geographical location; it encompasses both meanings. The Greek Ioudaioi were basically the descendants of the people of Judah, who worshipped the God of Israel as their patron deity and, by definition, lived according to the laws that the God of Israel had given his people.

- Those laws are contained in what Jews call the Torah, or the five books of Moses, the Pentateuch. The Greeks and Romans characterized the directives in the Torah as the ancestral laws of the Jews. They viewed them as ancient laws that were given to the Jews by their national deity.

- Recently, however, some scholars have begun to translate *Ioudaioi* as meaning only "Judeans." To some, this is controversial because this translation eliminates the religious aspect of ancient Judaism by emphasizing the geographical origin, and it removes Jews from the historical record. This problem of the translation is particularly acute in relation to the Gospel of John, which uses the term *Ioudaioi* far more than the other three Gospels combined.
  - In John, the Ioudaioi figure most prominently as Jesus's opponents, who created a murderous conspiracy to have Jesus crucified. In John 8:44, they are portrayed as children of the devil, who is the father of lies.

  - The scholar Adele Reinhartz observes, "The potent association between the Ioudaioi and the devil remains deeply embedded in anti-Semitic discourse to this day. Eliminating the Jews lets the Gospel of John off the hook for its role in the history of anti-Judaism and anti-Semitism."

Chronology of Our Course
- There is a custom among many Jews of calling a synagogue a temple, but in antiquity, a temple was literally the house of the deity. Only priests entered the temple in order to service the

In many ways, modern synagogues are the opposite of ancient temples, which were not meant to hold congregations of worshippers.

needs of the deity; everyone else stayed outside the temple building and congregated around an altar, where priests offered sacrifices to the deity. By contrast, synagogues, churches, and mosques today are intended to accommodate congregations of people for the purposes of prayer and worship.

- In this course, we will focus on the temple to the God of Israel, which was located on the Temple Mount in Jerusalem. In fact, there were two successive temples dedicated to the God of Israel.
  - The First Temple was constructed under Solomon's reign somewhere around 960 B.C. and destroyed by the Babylonians in 586 B.C. That timespan represents the First Temple period.

- The Second Temple was consecrated in 516 B.C., rebuilt around 20–10 B.C. by King Herod the Great, and destroyed by the Romans in 70 A.D. That timespan represents the Second Temple period.

- Chronologically, this course will begin with the story of the Israelites' flight from Egypt and the settlement of the 12 tribes of Israel and Canaan. Then, we will focus mainly on the Second Temple period, especially the late Second Temple period—that is, the 1st century B.C. and 2nd century A.D.: the time of Jesus.

Judaism and Other Ancient Religions

- Often, our view of ancient Judaism is distorted because we tend to remove it from its context and consider it to be different from other ancient religions. In fact, Judaism had many similarities with other ancient religions in the Mediterranean world and the Near East. For example, early Judaism had a temple that housed its deity, and priests offered sacrifices on an altar located outside the temple building.

- Eventually, however, Judaism mandated that there would be only one temple to the God of Israel, to be located on the Temple Mount in Jerusalem. This was an aspect that differed from other ancient religions. For example, there were temples to Athena located all around the ancient world, not just in Athens.
  - Another difference between Judaism and other ancient religions is that Judaism eventually prohibited the worship of other gods alongside the God of Israel. Furthermore, Judaism prohibited representing the God of Israel in physical form, in contrast to the use of cult statues found in other religions.

  - Another distinction between ancient Judaism and other religions is that the priesthood in Judaism was a caste system. In most other ancient religions, the priesthood was an office that could be bought and sold. Yet another difference was that Jews possessed a corpus of written laws, or sacred scripture, given to them by the God of Israel, instructing them on how to worship God and live their lives.

Monotheism and Monolatry

- We often refer to Judaism, Christianity, and Islam as monotheistic religions. *Monotheism*, a term that comes from the Greek, is the belief that only one deity exists. The term *monolatry*, in contrast, means the worship of only one god, while accepting the existence of other deities. In other words, a monolatrist is someone who acknowledges the existence of many other gods but worships only one god among that pantheon.

- In fact, monolatry is a more appropriate description of ancient Judaism than monotheism. Ancient Jews took for granted that there were many different deities that existed, but Judaism mandated that Jews could worship only the God of Israel, their chief deity. Selected passages from both the Old Testament and the New Testament support this position. For example, Psalm 86 says, "There is none like you among the gods, O Lord."

Theos Hypsistos in the Old Testament

- The Greek term *Theos Hypsistos* literally means "Highest God" or "God Most High." Ancient peoples applied this term to the chief deity in a pantheon. For example, in the Greek pantheon, Zeus was the chief deity; in the Roman pantheon, it was Jupiter.

- Interestingly, we sometimes find the term *Theos Hypsistos* applied to the God of Israel and used by both Jews and non-Jews alike. The term seems to be an equivalent of the Hebrew term El Elyon, which literally means "God Most High."

- We see these terms used in biblical passages. For example, Genesis 14:18–19 says, "King Melchizedek of Salem brought out bread and wine. He was priest of God Most High. He blessed him and said, 'Blessed be Abram by God Most High, Maker of heaven and earth.'" Similarly, in Daniel 2:47, we read, "The King said to Daniel, 'Truly, your God is God of gods and Lord of kings and a revealer of mysteries.'" This passage expresses the idea that the God of Israel is a chief deity among the pantheon of deities.

Theos Hypsistos in the New Testament

- Although the above passages come from the Hebrew Bible, or Old Testament, the concept of the God of Israel being a chief deity in a pantheon is also reflected in the New Testament. In Mark 5:7, we read, "And he shouted at the top of his voice, 'What have you to do with me, Jesus, Son of the Most High God?'"

- Similarly, in Luke 2:32 and 35 (and elsewhere in Luke), we see this same concept reflected: "He will be great and will be called the Son of the Most High." "The Holy Spirit will come upon you and the power of the Most High will overshadow you." The Most High God, the God of Israel, is above all other gods.

- In order to understand ancient Judaism, it is important to remember that the Jews were embedded in a world that was populated by peoples who worshipped many different gods. However, the Jewish God was conceived of as the chief deity, the Most High God of the people of Israel.

Suggested Reading
Goldenberg, *The Origins of Judaism*, chapter 1, "The Prehistory of Judaism."

Questions to Consider
1. What did the Greek term *Ioudaioi* (singular: *Ioudaios*) mean in antiquity, and why do scholars disagree about its translation?

2. What were the similarities and differences between ancient Judaism and other ancient religions in the Mediterranean world and Near East?

Lecture 2

Sacred Mountains and Law Giving in Judaism

According to ancient Judaism, there was no distinction between religion and politics—between the sacred and the profane—because Jewish life was governed by sacred law. The laws of the God of Israel were collected in the five books of Moses, called the Torah. Many of these laws concern how God wants the people to worship him; other laws govern the everyday lives of the Israelites. Furthermore, in Leviticus, the Holiness Code calls for all of Israel to emulate God's holiness in their everyday lives. In this lecture, we will discuss the importance of the Torah and examine the traditions surrounding the sacred mountain and the giving of the law.

A Religion of Laws
- In antiquity, the Jews were a people who came from the territory of Judah, worshipped the God of Israel as their deity, and lived according to the Torah—the laws the God of Israel gave his people. In other words, Jews were defined by both geography and religion.

- From a Jewish perspective, Christianity was a Jewish sect until its followers rejected the need to observe the laws in the Torah. This break occurred specifically when Paul extended his mission among the Gentiles without requiring them to undergo formal conversion to Judaism or to observe Jewish law. For example, the Gentiles were not required to undergo circumcision, keep dietary laws, or observe the Sabbath.

- Christianity is a creedal religion, which follows a creed, or set of fundamental beliefs; in contrast, Judaism is a religion of practice, or *praxis*. In Judaism, observing the law is a fundamental part of the religion.

Key Texts and Sources

- The Hebrew Bible, or Old Testament, contains three groups of writings: the Torah, Prophets, and Writings. The Torah, or the five books of Moses, comprises Genesis, Exodus, Leviticus, Numbers, and Deuteronomy. The Hebrew term for the Hebrew Bible is Tanakh, an acronym derived from the names Torah, Prophets, and Writings.

- A fundamental body of literature that will inform these lectures is the Apocrypha, which means "hidden books" or "hidden works." These are books that were included in the Catholic Bible but not in the Hebrew or Protestant Bible. Examples of apocryphal writings include 1 Maccabees, 2 Maccabees, and Tobit.

- Another key category of biblical literature is called Pseudepigrapha, which literally means "false writings." The authors of these works hid their identities under other names in order to give their works greater authority. Pseudepigrapha are Jewish religious works from around the time of Jesus that were not included in the Catholic, Hebrew, or Protestant Bible. Examples of Pseudepigrapha are the books of Enoch and Jubilees.

- Many works in the Apocrypha and Pseudepigrapha are represented among the Dead Sea Scrolls, which are writings dating from the 2nd and 1st centuries B.C. that were deposited in caves around Qumran, on the northwest shore of the Dead Sea.

- Perhaps the single most significant source of information for these lectures is the work of Flavius Josephus, a Jewish historian who lived in the 1st century A.D. Josephus wrote a series of historical works that provide much of our information about the Jews in the time of Jesus, up to the destruction of the Second Temple by the Romans in the year 70.

- Another source of information is rabbinic literature, a corpus of work associated with a group of Jewish sages, or rabbis, who lived in the centuries after the time of Jesus. Their legal rulings, as well as other literature that they produced, were eventually written down and collected in such works as the Talmud.

Exodus from Egypt
- To trace the origins of the Israelites, we begin with the Exodus from Egypt, described in Exodus 12:29–32. Today, many scholars believe that if there was an Exodus, it consisted of a very small group of people who later became the core of the Israelite tribes.

- If we follow the biblical account, sometime around 1200 B.C., these Israelite tribes entered Canaan, which is roughly the area today of modern Israel and the Palestinian territories. The Israelites settled in the mountainous interior part of the country.

- At the same time as the arrival of the Israelites, the Philistines settled along the coast. The Canaanites continued to live in the north, in the area of modern Lebanon, which in antiquity was called Phoenicia. They became known as the Phoenicians. Other peoples living in that area include the Ammonites, Moabites, and Edomites.

- The Israelites came into conflict with both the Canaanites and the Philistines. For example, 1 Samuel tells us: "Now, it happened, in those days, that the Philistines mustered against Israel for war, and Israel went out to meet the Philistines in battle."

A Celestial Deity
- The giving of the law to Moses at Mount Sinai is one of the most significant events in the history of the Israelites. While the Israelites were wandering in the desert, the God of Israel gave the law, the Torah, to Moses at Mount Sinai, as described in Exodus 19–24.

- In antiquity, gods inhabited different places. Celestial deities lived in heaven, while *chthonic deities* lived underground. Each type of god was worshipped differently. For example, worship of

In order to encounter the presence of the God of Israel—a celestial deity—Moses was instructed to go to the top of Mount Sinai.

a celestial deity involved burning meat or another offering on an altar, allowing the smoke to rise up to the god in the heavens above. However, worship of a chthonic deity would involve pouring water or wine into the ground.

- The God of Israel was a celestial deity. To communicate with this god, worshippers had to get as close to him as possible. It is not a coincidence, then, that in order to reach the God of Israel, Moses had to go to the top of Mount Sinai.

- The concept of the sacred mountain was quite common in antiquity. For example, the Greek gods dwelled on top of Mount Olympus. Another example of a sacred mountain was the Temple Mount in Jerusalem, Mount Moriah, where both the First Temple and Second Temple were built.

- The concept of a sacred mountain also occurs in Christian tradition—for example, the Sermon on the Mount, where Jesus reinterprets the old law. Matthew 5:1–3 reads: "When Jesus saw the crowds, he went up the mountain. And after he sat down, his disciples came to him. Then he began to speak, and taught them, saying, blessed are the poor in spirit for theirs is the kingdom of Heaven."
    - Interestingly, the Sermon on the Mount contains six antitheses that contrast Israelite law with Jesus's teachings. For example, Exodus 20:14 warns against committing adultery. However, in Matthew 5:27, Jesus says, "You have heard that it was said, you shall not commit adultery. But I say to you that everyone who looks at a woman with lust has already committed adultery with her in his heart."

    - In fact, the Sermon on the Mount contains a very specific example in which Jesus takes the old law and reinterprets it as a new law. Certainly, this must be understood against the background of the giving of the law originally on Mount Sinai to Moses.

- The concept of the sacred mountain is reflected in another significant episode in the New Testament—the transfiguration of Jesus.
    - In Mark 9:1–4, we read: "Six days later, Jesus took with him Peter, and James, and John and led them up a high mountain, apart, by themselves. And he was transfigured before them, and his clothes became dazzling white such as no one on Earth could bleach them. And there appeared to them Elijah with Moses, where they were talking with Jesus."

    - In a dramatic moment, Moses appears, representing the law, the Torah. Elijah represents the prophets. In the Sermon on the Mount, recorded in Matthew 5:17, Jesus says, "Do not think that I have come to abolish the law or the prophets. I have come not to abolish, but to fulfill." Jesus builds on the concept of sacred mountain and law that is deeply embedded within Judaism to create a new law.

Suggested Reading

Cohen, *From the Maccabees to the Mishnah*, chapter 3, "The Jewish 'Religion': Practices and Beliefs," pp. 60–79.

Nickelsburg, *Ancient Judaism and Christian Origins*, chapter 1, "Scripture and Tradition."

Questions to Consider

1. At what point did Christianity cease to be a Jewish sect?

2. How do Judaism and Christianity differ with regard to matters of faith and practice?

Lecture 3: The United and Divided Israelite Kingdoms

In this lecture, we follow the transformation of the Israelites from a tribal society into a monarchy under the reigns of David and Solomon and learn how the United Monarchy eventually dissolved as a result of tensions between the northern and southern tribes. We will analyze the biases and perspectives of the authors of the Hebrew Bible and conclude by examining the origin of the New Testament references to Beelzeboul, ruler of the demons.

King David

- Sometime around 1030 B.C., the Israelite tribes united together under the rule of Saul. In 1 Samuel 14:52, we read that there was constant fighting against the Philistines during Saul's reign. This is the background for David's rise to power. In one battle, David kills the Philistine Goliath with a sling and stone. According to the biblical accounts, Saul and his sons lost their lives in battle against the Philistines.

- David succeeded Saul as king sometime around 1000 B.C. David then expanded the Israelite kingdom and ruled for 40 years. One of his most significant accomplishments was to capture Jerusalem, in the heart of the hill country that had been settled by the Israelites. But in the 200 years since the Israelites had first arrived, they had not been able to take Jerusalem from its native population, the Jebusites. It had remained a foreign enclave in the heart of Israelite territory.

- David made Jerusalem the capital of his kingdom and called it the City of David. In addition to making Jerusalem the political capital of the Israelite kingdom, David also brought the Ark of the Covenant to Jerusalem, thereby making the worship of the God of Israel the unifying bond of the 12 tribes.

King Solomon

- Sometime around 970 B.C., David died and was succeeded to the throne by his son, Solomon. Solomon used diplomatic means to cement political alliances, including marrying female members of the ruling families of neighboring peoples. The peoples represented by the ruling families were those bordering the Israelites on all sides—Ammonites, Edomites, and Moabites.

- In addition to these politically motivated marriages or alliances, Solomon also is known for having built the First Temple of the God of Israel on the Temple Mount in Jerusalem. The temple housed the Ark of the Covenant, which David had brought to the city. We are told in 1 Kings 6:1 that in the fourth year of Solomon's reign over Israel, he built the house of the Lord. Notice the reference to the temple as a house; it was the house in which the God of Israel dwelled.

- Solomon's death in about 930 B.C. brought to an end a period in the history of Israel that is referred to as the United Kingdom or the United Monarchy. During this time, the 12 Israelite tribes were unified under the rule of a single king.

Solomon's many marriages were clearly politically motivated; he took as wives the daughters of the ruling families of Ammon, Edom, and Moab—ancient kingdoms surrounding the Israelites.

Archaeological Evidence
- Some scholars debate whether David and Solomon existed at all and, instead, speculate that they are legendary or mythical figures that were fabricated by later biblical writers to create a mythology, a basis for the establishment of the Israelites.

- The accuracy of the biblical descriptions of the United Monarchy are lively topics for debate in scholarship today. One of the problems facing scholars is that even by the most optimistic estimates, the biblical text was not written down and edited until centuries after the time of David and Solomon. The archaeological evidence is not unequivocal either. Just as the text can be interpreted in different ways, so can the archaeological evidence.

- In the 1990s, a stele (inscribed stone) was found at Tel Dan, in the northern part of Israel. This stele dates to the second half of the 9th century B.C., the century after the time of David. Significantly, the stele mentions the house of David, meaning the dynasty of King David. This means that within a century of when David is thought to have lived, people were tracing their ancestry back to him—which would argue that there was in fact a historical David.

Dissolution of the United Monarchy
- When Solomon died, the United Monarchy dissolved and split into a northern and a southern half. The transformation of Israelite society into an early state and a unified monarchy had always been resisted by the northern tribes, known as the house of Israel. The northern tribes resented the southern tribes, who held superior positions in the civil government and the military. In fact, the capital of the United Monarchy was at Jerusalem, in the south.

- Now there were two independent and separate kingdoms, each with its own political capital and king. In the Northern kingdom of Israel, the capital was Samaria. In the Southern kingdom of Judah, the capital remained in Jerusalem.

- Against this background of conflict and tension between the northern and southern tribes, there was significant disagreement over how to properly worship Yahweh, the God of Israel. Essentially, the dispute centered on the issue of inclusive versus exclusive Yahwism.

Biases of the Biblical Writers

- In analyzing the Hebrew Bible, we must account for the biases of the writers and editors of that work. Creators of the Hebrew Bible were pro-Judah and anti-Israel—that is, pro-south and anti-north. Further, they favored exclusive rather than inclusive Yahwism. Inclusive Yahwists allowed the veneration of other gods alongside Yahweh but worshipped Yahweh, the god of Israel, as their national god. By contrast, exclusive Yahwists did not tolerate the worship of any other gods than Yahweh. Of course, that perspective is the one that eventually won out.

- Another predisposition of the biblical writers is that they favored the centralization of the cult—that is, they believed that there was only one place where one may offer sacrifices to the God of Israel. The biblical writers condemned kings who established sanctuaries outside of Jerusalem to worship the God of Israel.

- Centralization of the cult in Jerusalem placed religion under the control of the high priests serving in the Jerusalem Temple. What's more, centralization of the cult favored the kingdom of Judah, which controlled Jerusalem.

The 10 Lost Tribes

- We see the bias of the biblical authors reflected in various biblical passages. For example, Jeroboam, who succeeded Solomon as the king of Israel in the north, established an alternative sanctuary in the territory of the Northern kingdom. He took two calves of gold and set up one in Bethel and the other in Dan. This became a sin to Israel.

Lecture 3—The United and Divided Israelite Kingdoms | 19

- Omari, a king of Israel after Jeroboam, secured an alliance with the Phoenician king of Tyre by marrying his son Ahab to Ithobaal's daughter Jezebel. Notice that Ithobaal and Jezebel both have a similar component in their names: *baal* or *bel*. Baal was the national god of the Canaanites and the Phoenicians; thus, embedded in the names of Ithobaal and Jezebel is the name of the national deity.

- King Ahab (c. 872–851 B.C.) was actually a capable king under whose rule the kingdom of Israel prospered. However, Ahab is presented in an extremely negative light in the Hebrew Bible because the writers or editors were anti-north and anti-Israel, and because Ahab was an inclusive Yahwist, like other members of the Samaria aristocracy. What's more, Ahab's wife Jezebel aggressively promoted the worship of Baal in Israel.

- Ahab reigned over Israel and Samaria for 22 years, but he provoked the God of Israel by also worshipping Baal. After Ahab died, the members of his family were executed during a bloody purge, and Jezebel was put to death.

- About two centuries later, the Northern kingdom of Israel fell. At this time, the dominant power in the ancient Near East was the Assyrian Empire, based in the northern part of modern Iraq. In 722 B.C., the Assyrians conquered the Northern kingdom of Israel and sent the people of Israel into exile. This is the source of the story of the 10 lost tribes.

From Baal to Beelzebub
- Analyzing the worship of Baal, the patron deity of the Canaanites and the Phoenicians, leads us to a figure who is connected with the New Testament accounts: Beelzeboul. In Mark 3:22, we read, "And the scribes who came down from Jerusalem said, he has Beelzeboul. And by the ruler of the demons, he cast out demons." In other words, in the New Testament, Beelzeboul is the ruler of the demons.

- Consider the god Baal, the chief deity of the Canaanites and the Phoenicians. The word *baal* literally means "lord" or "master." *Baalezebul* originally meant "Baal the prince," as in the chief deity. Beelzeboul is a variation on that name.

- The story of Beelzebub is found in 2 Kings 1:2–3. This story reflects the condemnation by the biblical writers of inclusive Yahwism in the time of Ahab's son Ahaziah:

    Ahaziah had fallen through the lattice in his upper chamber in Samaria, and lay injured; so he sent messengers, telling them, "Go, inquire of Baal-zebub, the god of Ekron, whether I shall recover from this injury." But the angel of the Lord said to Elijah the Tishbite, "Get up, go to meet the messengers of the king of Samaria, and say to them, 'Is it because there is no God in Israel that you are going to inquire of Baal-zebub, the god of Ekron?'"

- Ekron was one of the cities of the Philistine pentapolis, and Beelzebub was the god who was being consulted. The name Beelzebub is very close to Baalezebul or Beelzeboul. *Beelzebub*, translated literally, means "lord of the flies." In effect, the biblical writers created an intentional corruption and a deliberate pun or play on that name—turning a prince into the lord of the flies.

Suggested Reading
Goldenberg, *The Origins of Judaism*, chapter 2, "The Beginnings of Monotheism."

Questions to Consider
1. What are some of the current debates concerning David and his kingdom?

2. What is inclusive versus exclusive Yahwism?

Lecture 4 — The Destruction of Solomon's Temple

In this lecture, we follow the history of the kingdom of Judah until its conquest by the Babylonians and the destruction of Solomon's Temple. The foretelling of the destruction of the First Temple by earlier prophets foreshadowed Jesus's prediction that the Second Temple would be destroyed. The Gospel accounts that describe conversations between Jesus and his disciples about the end of days and place Jesus on the Mount of Olives draw on significant biblical traditions connected with the earlier Israelite prophets.

Reforms of King Josiah

- One of the most celebrated kings of Judah was King Josiah, who ruled from approximately 640 to 609 B.C. Josiah was loved by the biblical writers because of his religious reforms, which reasserted the centrality of the Temple of Jerusalem and its priesthood and eliminated local sanctuaries. In other words, because Josiah's reforms were perfectly in keeping with the preferences and views of the biblical writers, they described him in glowing terms.

- According to one biblical passage: "Then the king commanded Hilkiah the high priest to bring out of the temple of the Lord all the vessels that were made for the Baal, and the Asherah, and for all the host of the heavens. And he burned them outside Jerusalem in the lime kilns by the Kidron and carried away their ashes to Bethel."

- Notice that Josiah is clearing out objects of worship to gods other than the God of Israel in the Jerusalem Temple. This act demonstrates the continuing tension between inclusive and exclusive Yahwism among the Israelites, even in the 8th and 7th centuries B.C.

- The passage continues: "Moreover he brought the Asherah from the house of the Lord outside Jerusalem to the Kidron Valley and burned it at the Kidron Valley and ground to powder and cast the powder of it upon the graves of the common people. Furthermore, he tore down the houses of the devotees of the fertility cult, which were in the house of the Lord, where the women wove tunics for the Asherah."

- *Asherah* is an enigmatic term debated by scholars. Some think that the Asherah refers to a female consort of the God of Israel. It was, of course, typical in antiquity for male deities to have female companions.

- The centerpiece of Josiah's reform was the discovery, or reputed discovery, of a book of law, which came to be called the Book of Deuteronomy, during work on the temple building in Jerusalem. This law is called a "Second Law" because it basically reformulates and restates many of the laws that are in the first four books of Moses. Therefore, Josiah's reform is called the Deuteronomistic reform.

Armageddon

- Josiah's assertion of the centrality of Jerusalem served to unify the country and strengthen the central government. Unfortunately, however, Josiah died an untimely death, at the hands of the Egyptians.

- In the ancient Near East, Babylonia was an emerging power; and, at the time of Josiah, Assyria, Egypt, and Babylonia were jockeying for position. The Egyptians were trying to bolster the weaker power, Assyria, against the stronger, emerging power, Babylonia; thus, the Egyptians sent an army out to support the Assyrians. To travel to Assyria, the Egyptians had to pass through the area where Josiah's kingdom was located.

- According to the biblical account, "In the year 609 B.C., the Egyptian pharaoh Necho II set out with a large army and marched northwards." As the Egyptian army was crossing the mountain pass at the foot of Megiddo (a large biblical tell), Josiah confronted them, and Necho captured and killed him.

- Because of Josiah's reforms, the biblical writers viewed him as a second David: "Josiah was eight years old when he began to reign. He reigned 31 years in Jerusalem. He did what was right in the sight of the Lord and walked in all the way of his father David. He did not turn aside to the right or to the left." Because the biblical writers directly compared Josiah to King David, Josiah's death was a disaster that also put an end to the hopes of a revived kingdom of Judah.

- Interestingly, Josiah's death occurred at the site of Megiddo. Megiddo guards the outlet of a crucial mountain pass in the center of Israel. In antiquity, many significant battles were fought there. Eventually, Josiah's death at Megiddo became identified as the site of the ultimate battle at the end of days, as expressed in the Revelation of John 16:14–16: "They are demon spirits that perform wonders, and they go out to the kings all over the world to muster them for battle on the great day of God Almighty. So they mustered the kings at the place called, in Hebrew, Armageddon."

- The Greek word *Armageddon* actually comes from the Hebrew words *Har Megiddo*, meaning "Mount Megiddo." In Greek, *Har Megiddo* became *Har-Magedon*. In English, it became *Armageddon*.

The Babylonian Exile
- After Josiah's death, the Babylonians began to conduct a series of military campaigns against the kingdom of Judah, exiling the inhabitants of Judah to Babylonia. All of this culminated in the year 586 B.C., when the Babylonians besieged Jerusalem for 18 months. That siege ended with the fall of Jerusalem and the destruction of Solomon's Temple.

- The king of Judah at that time was Zedekiah. He was captured by the Babylonians while trying to escape the city under the cover of night. His sons were put to death in front of his eyes, and he was then blinded so that the last sight he ever saw was the death of his sons.

- The destruction of Jerusalem and the fall of the kingdom of Judah in 586 B.C. mark the end of the First Temple period and the beginning of the Babylonian Exile. The Babylonian Exile lasted from 586 to 539 B.C. It is commemorated in a number of memorable passages in the Bible, including Psalm 37: "By the rivers of Babylon, there we sat down and wept when we remembered Zion. How could we sing the songs of the Lord in a foreign land? If I forget you, O Jerusalem, may my right hand fail me. May my tongue cleave to my palate if I do not remember you, if I set not Jerusalem above my highest joy."

Foreshadowing the Destruction of the Second Temple

- The destruction of the First Temple, Solomon's Temple, was a deeply traumatic event for the Judeans. What's more, this event was drawn upon by later authors referring to the destruction of the Second Temple. The destruction of the First Temple became a foreshadowing of the destruction of the Second Temple.

- This foreshadowing figures prominently when we talk about Jesus and the Gospel accounts because, according to Mark, Matthew, and Luke, Jesus foretold the destruction of the Second Temple. For example, a critical passage in the Gospel accounts tells us: "As he came out of the temple, one of his disciples said to him, 'Look, teacher, what large stones and what large buildings.' Then Jesus asked him, 'Do you see these great buildings? Not one stone will be left here upon another. All will be thrown down.'"

- Of course, a key theme throughout the Gospel accounts is Jesus being cast in the light of a biblical prophet. It is not coincidental, therefore, that earlier Israelite prophets had reportedly foretold the destruction of the First Temple. Thus, when we see Jesus reportedly foretelling the destruction of the Second Temple, he is doing much the same thing that earlier Israelite prophets had reportedly done with regard to the First Temple, following in a biblical tradition.

- For example, consider this passage from Jeremiah: "Therefore, I will do to the house that is called by My name, in which you trust, and to the place that I gave to you and to your ancestors, just what I did to Shiloh." Similarly, in Micah, we find: "Therefore, because of you Zion shall be plowed as a field. Jerusalem shall become a heap of ruins and the mountain of the house, a wooded height."

- In addition, there were other works later on, aside from those of the Gospel authors, that used this sort of evocative language of the destruction of the First Temple to refer to the destruction of the Second Temple. One of these works was the Fourth Book of Ezra or the Second Book of Esdras—an apocalyptic work written in the 90s A.D. The writer evokes the destruction of the First Temple, but what he's really talking about is the destruction of the Second Temple.

Significance of the Mount of Olives

- One of the Gospel accounts, Mark 24:3, describes Jesus sitting on the Mount of Olives: "When he was sitting on the Mount of Olives, the disciples came to him privately saying, 'Tell us when will this be and what will be the sign of your coming and the end of the age?'"

- Jesus's place on the Mount of Olives is crucial to understanding the significance of this passage. The Mount of Olives is located to the east of Jerusalem, across the Kidron Valley from the Temple Mount. Jesus is sitting on top of this mountain overlooking the city. According to Ezekiel 11:23, the Mount of Olives was the place where the glory of God went after departing the Temple.

The Mount of Olives had great significance in the biblical tradition; it was the place where the glory of God went after departing the Temple and where the Messiah was expected to appear.

- The Mount of Olives has further significance because, according to biblical tradition, it is also the place where the Messiah was expected to appear. In Zachariah 14:4–5, the author says, "On that day, His feet shall stand on the Mount of Olives, which lies before Jerusalem on the east, and the Mount of Olives shall be split into from east to west by a very wide valley, so that one half of the Mount shall withdraw northward and the other half southward. Then the Lord my God will come and all the holy ones with him."

Suggested Reading
Goldenberg, *The Origins of Judaism*, chapter 3, "The Book and the People."

Questions to Consider
1. Why did the biblical writers like Josiah?

2. What is the significance of the Mount of Olives in Jewish tradition?

Lecture

5   The Jewish and Samaritan Schism

By 586 B.C., the Babylonians had conquered the kingdom of Judah, destroyed the city of Jerusalem, and sent the inhabitants of Judah into exile in Babylonia, beginning a period in Jewish history known as the Babylonian Exile. The Babylonian Exile ended in 539 B.C., when Cyrus, king of Persia, issued an edict allowing the Judeans to return to Jerusalem and rebuild their temple. In this lecture, we survey the return of the exiled Judeans to Jerusalem under the Persians, which led to the schism between the Jews and the Samaritans. We conclude with the account of the Good Samaritan in Luke and the story of Jesus and the Samaritan woman in John.

The End of the Babylonian Exile

- According to the author of Ezra in the Hebrew Bible, it was the God of Israel who caused Cyrus to issue the edict allowing the exiled Judeans to return to their homeland and rebuild God's house in Jerusalem. What's more, the God of Israel was identified as the God in Jerusalem.

- Interestingly, the Persians had a political policy of repatriating conquered peoples—unlike other Near Eastern powers, such as the Assyrians and Babylonians, who typically exiled those they conquered.

- By repatriating native peoples to their homelands, the Persians were hoping to win their loyalty and allegiance. This was certainly the case of the dispersed Babylonian Jews; they were deeply grateful to be able to return to Jerusalem and rebuild the temple.

- It is crucial to remember, however, that many of the exiled Babylonian Jews never returned to Jerusalem. Many of them had become well-established in the intervening decades and chose to remain where they were, forming the core of a flourishing Diaspora community in Babylonia for many centuries.

Eber-Nari

- The Persian Empire was vast, stretching from today's Iran and Asia Minor to Egypt and encompassing modern Israel and the Palestinian territories. In order to govern such a huge area, the Persians divided their empire into smaller units called *satrapies*. Each satrapy was ruled by a governor called a *satrap*.

- Judea, formerly the kingdom of Judah, was part of a large satrapy called Eber-Nari, meaning the land "beyond the river." From the Persian perspective, the region was located to the west of the Euphrates River.

- The state to the north of Judea was Samaria, which had been the capital of the biblical kingdom of Israel much earlier. The inhabitants of Samaria were Samarians, later known as the Samaritans.

Ezra and Nehemiah

- The exiled Jewish community of Babylonia greeted Cyrus as a liberator and saw his work as fulfilling a divine purpose in national redemption. Successive waves of exiles returned to Judea over the course of the decades after Cyrus issued his edict. The city of Jerusalem was resettled, and the temple was rebuilt on the Temple Mount. Construction of the Second Temple was completed in 516 B.C.

- Against this background of repatriation and rebuilding of the city of Jerusalem, we note two key biblical figures, Ezra and Nehemiah. Ezra was a scribe knowledgeable in the laws of the Torah who came to Jerusalem in 458 B.C. He had a commission from the Persian king Artaxerxes to implement Jewish law as the law of Judea. Therefore, under royal command, Jewish law—the laws in the five books of Moses—became the law of the land of Judea.

- Nehemiah came to Jerusalem in 445 B.C. and served two terms as a governor, until 424 B.C. Nehemiah, a Jew, had attained a high office in the Persian administration: cupbearer to the king.

It was under Nehemiah's administration of Jerusalem that the walls of the city were rebuilt.

From the Israelite Religion to Judaism

- During the period of repatriation, the Israelite religion was transformed into Judaism. During the Babylonian Exile, the tribal structure of Israelite society had broken down. Before 586 B.C., those who worshipped the God of Israel were members of the Israelite tribes. If you were born into one of the Israelite tribes or married into one of them, then by definition, you worshipped the God of Israel as your national deity. But after 586 B.C., the tribal system ceased to exist, which led to a significant change in worship.

- In his writings, Ezra demanded an intact genealogy, or pure bloodline, for participation in the worship of the God of Israel. It is not a coincidence that the Book of Ezra opens with lists of the genealogies of the returning Judean exiles.

- The emphasis on pure bloodlines and genealogy is an upper-class, elite concern. In fact, only the upper-class Judeans had been sent into exile, because the goal was to disrupt the local power base. When the Persians allowed the exiled Babylonian Jews to return, those clans who came back were basically the upper classes, who had preserved their genealogies.

- Ezra forbade Judeans who had intermarried with non-Jews to participate in the cult of the Jerusalem Temple, unless they sent away their foreign wives and children. This was a new feature of the religion; intermarriage had not been a concern of the 12 tribes before that.

- Scholars distinguish between the two phases by referring to Israelite religion as the religion of the 12 tribes of Israel, versus Judaism, which was the religion of the returning Judean exiles.

Schism with the Samaritans

- The new features of Judaism led to a significant schism between the Judeans and Samaritans. When the exiled Judeans came back from Babylonia to rebuild Jerusalem and the temple, the descendants of the Israelites in the north wished to participate in rebuilding the temple. But because many of these northerners had intermarried with other peoples, according to Ezra's prohibition, they were not allowed to participate in worshipping the God of Israel in the Jerusalem Temple.

- These northerners were located around the city of Samaria. Ezra's prohibition led to a split between the descendants of the Israelites to the north and the Judeans to the south. This schism led to the formation of the group called the Samaritans.

- The Samaritans established an alternative sanctuary on their own sacred mountain, Mount Gerizim, where they eventually built their own temple dedicated to the God of Israel. The Samaritans viewed themselves as the true Israel; they claimed descent from the old Joseph tribes of the north, Ephraim and Manasseh. The Samaritans also had their own version of sacred Hebrew scripture, the Samaritan Pentateuch.

- Like many people who are closely related, the Judeans and the Samaritans fought bitterly, because they were struggling over a common heritage. In the eyes of the Judeans, the Samaritans were schismatics.

- One of the governors of Samaria under the Persians was a man named Sanballat I. At the same time, Tobiah, a Jew, was governor of Ammon. According to the Hebrew Bible, both Sanballat I and Tobiah viewed Nehemiah's rebuilding of the walls of the city of Jerusalem as a threat. A passage in Nehemiah (4:6–7) reflects tensions between the governors of these adjacent districts, who were concerned that no one in the area should become more powerful than another.

- According to the historian Flavius Josephus, Sanballat III, who was the grandson of Sanballat I, lived at the time of the conquest of Alexander the Great, in the year 332 B.C. Sanballat III, the governor of Samaria, supported Alexander, and in return, Alexander granted the Samaritans permission to build a temple on Mount Gerizim.

Biblical Stories of Samaritans
- The schism between the Judeans and the Samaritans sheds interesting light on the story of the Good Samaritan, recounted in the Gospel of Luke (10:30–34). As you recall, a man is left beaten on the side of the road by robbers, and both a priest and a Levite see him but cross to the other side of the road to avoid helping him. Finally, a Samaritan happens upon the man, dresses his wounds, and takes him to an inn.
  - When we read that passage today, we think that the point is to show the immorality of the priest and the Levite versus the Good Samaritan. But in fact, in this passage, the priest and the Levite are strictly following biblical Hebrew law. According to these laws, it is forbidden to enter the presence of the God of Israel when one is in a state of ritual impurity, and the worst kind of ritual impurity is coming into contact with a human corpse.

  - In detouring around what they thought was a corpse, the priest and the Levite were following biblical law. But the author of the story makes the point that the truly moral person here was the Samaritan, viewed as a schismatic by the Jews.

- In another story, recounted in the Gospel of John, Jesus encounters a Samaritan woman at a well and asks for a drink.
  - According to John 4: "The Samaritan woman said, 'How is it that you, a Jew, ask a drink of me, a woman of Samaria?' The woman said to him, 'Sir, I see that you are a prophet. Our ancestors worshipped on this mountain, but you say that the place where people must worship is in Jerusalem.'"

The story of the Good Samaritan in the Gospel of Luke is more clearly understood against the backdrop of the schism between the Judeans and the Samaritans.

- The Gospel passages in Luke and John relate both directly and indirectly to the schism between the Jews and the Samaritans—a schism that occurred against the backdrop of the returning exiles from Babylonia who reestablished themselves in Jerusalem.

Suggested Reading

Cohen, *From the Maccabees to the Mishnah*, "From Pre-exilic Israel to Second Temple Judaism," pp. 20–24.

VanderKam, *An Introduction to Early Judaism*, chapter 1, "The Time of the Second Temple," pp. 1–11.

Questions to Consider

1. What is the difference between Israelite religion and early Judaism?

2. Who are the Samaritans?

Lecture 6

The Jewish Diaspora and the Golden Rule

In this lecture, we examine evidence of the ancient Jewish Diaspora communities in Assyria, Babylonia, Persia, and Egypt through literary works, such as the books of Tobit and Esther. We conclude with a discussion of the Golden Rule, a version of which occurs in Tobit, whose meaning was the subject of debate among Jews in the time of Jesus.

The Book of Tobit

- The Book of Tobit is an apocryphal book, which means that it is included in the Catholic Bible but not in the Jewish or Protestant canons of sacred scripture. The theme of Tobit is that God is with us, even in the midst of trouble and suffering; the book tells a story of hope and deliverance.

- In the story, Tobit is an Israelite exile in Assyria who has been punished by blinding for his righteous deeds (burying the dead). Far away, Sarah, who is a distant relative of Tobit, has been married seven times, and each time, her husband was killed on their wedding night by a demon who was in love with her. Both Tobit and Sarah pray for death as a release from their troubles.

- God responds by sending the angel Raphael, whose name literally means "God has healed." Raphael uses Tobiah, Tobit's son, as an agent to drive off the demon from Sarah and heal Tobit's blindness. Tobiah then marries Sarah. The moral of the story is that God rewards the pious, even if they must suffer first.

- This tale sounds like the story of Job, but with several important distinctions. Whereas in Job, the individual suffers; in Tobit, the suffering is collective. That is, exile and dispersion are God's punishment for Israel's sins. But the punishment is not final. The return from dispersion will have as its focus proper pan-Israelite worship in a rebuilt Jerusalem.

- The author of Tobit reaffirms the universal sovereignty of the God of Israel and God's presence among the dispersed. The message is that despite being outside the land of Israel, God's people are to maintain their identity and continue to worship the God of Israel.

The Book of Esther

- Tobit was probably written in the Diaspora, after 516 B.C., when the Second Temple was consecrated. A likely date is somewhere between 250 and 200 B.C. for the composition of this work. A number of Jewish works from the Second Temple period recount stories of Diaspora Jews and Diaspora Jewish life and provide evidence of Jews' occupying high positions in the service of foreign kings and rulers.

- One of these works is the Book of Esther, which is included in the Hebrew Bible. This work is set in the days of a king called Ahasuerus. Today, scholars identify King Ahasuerus as the Persian King Xerxes I, who ruled from 486 to 465 B.C. Xerxes I is probably best known as the Persian king who invaded Greece in 480 B.C.

- The story of Esther begins when Queen Vashti, the wife of King Ahasuerus, falls out of favor with the king. This sets in motion a search for a new wife for the king, eventually leading to Esther, a Jew, who becomes queen. The dramatic events that lie at the heart of this story focus on Esther and her cousin Mordecai foiling an attempt by the king's evil advisor Haman to exterminate the Jews. The series of events that culminates with the salvation of the Jews from Haman is commemorated by the Jewish holiday of Purim.

- Although the story of Esther does not appear to be historically based, it does portray a Jewish woman rising to the highest possible position within a conquering empire. Consider Nehemiah, whom we discussed in the last lecture. Nehemiah was cupbearer to the king. Stories such as these provide evidence that Jews living in the Diaspora prospered and were able to attain high office in the administrations of foreign kingdoms.

Jewish Diaspora in Egypt

- In addition to areas in the east, there was also a significant Jewish Diaspora in Egypt. In fact, the author of Jeremiah mentions the migration of Judeans to Egypt, including Jeremiah himself in the aftermath of the fall of Jerusalem in 586 B.C. We know from various sources that there was a significant Jewish military colony at a site called Elephantine, which was an island opposite Aswan.

- The Jews at Elephantine were part of a military force in charge of guarding Egypt's border with Nubia. The site is a crucial source of information about the Jewish Diaspora because an archive of documents was discovered there, consisting of more than 100 Aramaic papyri that date between 495 and 399 B.C.

- From the papyri, we learn that the Jews at Elephantine had a temple where they worshipped a god called YHW—obviously the same deity as Yahweh, the God of Israel. This is an example of a temple dedicated to the God of Israel that is not located on the Temple Mount in Jerusalem. And unlike the case of the Samaritan temple on Mount Gerizim, which was also dedicated to the God of Israel, the temple at Elephantine was never condemned as schismatic by Jews.

- In 411 or 410 B.C., the temple at Elephantine was destroyed by local Egyptian priests, who had taken advantage of the fact that the local Persian satrap was away on business. Following the temple's destruction, the local Jewish population of Elephantine tried to muster support for rebuilding the temple. They wrote a number of letters to various people, among them the high priest in Jerusalem and the governor of Samaria.

The Golden Rule in the Old Testament
- The Book of Tobit is an excellent illustration of the debates among Jews in the time of Jesus regarding the formulation of the Golden Rule. Tobit 4:15 contains a negative formulation of the Golden Rule. Specifically, it says, "And what you hate, do not do to anyone."

- The original formulation of the Golden Rule goes back to Leviticus 19:16–18, which says, "You shall not go around as a slanderer or tale bearer among your people, and you shall not profit by the blood of your neighbor. I am the Lord. You shall not hate in your heart any one of your kin. You shall reprove your neighbor, or you will incur guilt yourself. You shall not take vengeance or bear a grudge against any of your people, but you shall love your neighbor as yourself. I am the Lord."

- The Golden Rule was understood differently by various Jewish groups and sects. We know from the Dead Sea Scrolls that one sect understood "your people" and "your kin" as referring only to other members of the sect. Therefore, they were obligated to hate all others, including all other Jews.

- The Jewish sages who lived in the centuries following the destruction of the Second Temple in the year 70 A.D. interpreted "your people" and "your kin" as meaning all of Israel, even sinners, and identified the adversaries as Gentiles.

The Golden Rule in the New Testament
- According to the Gospel of Mark (12:29–31), Jesus regarded the injunction to love your neighbor as yourself as the second most important commandment. When a scribe asked Jesus which commandment was most important, he replied, "The first is hear, oh Israel, the Lord our God, the Lord is one. You shall love the Lord your God with all your heart and with all your soul and with all your might and with all your strength. The second is this. You

Jesus's formulation of the Golden Rule in the Gospel of Matthew reflects part of a larger debate among Jews at the time regarding the interpretation of this commandment.

shall love your neighbor as yourself. There is no other commandment greater than these."

- Matthew 5:43–48 reports that Jesus included even one's enemies among those who should be loved. This is from the Sermon on the Mount: "You have heard it was said, you shall love your neighbor and hate your enemy. But I say to you, love your enemies, and pray for those who persecute you, so that you may be children of your Father in Heaven."

- Here, Jesus is asking his followers to go beyond what is required and to love not only their neighbors but also their enemies. Thus, this passage in Matthew shows that Leviticus 19 generally was understood by Jews in this period as meaning that one should love one's neighbors and hate one's enemies, however they are defined.

- Jesus's statement, therefore, should be understood in the context of a wider debate among Jews regarding the interpretation of the Golden Rule in the time of Jesus. Interestingly, in Jesus's view, you shouldn't love only your neighbors but everyone, even your enemies. In other words, Jesus's response to the debate is that you are not supposed to hate anybody. You are supposed to love everyone, including Gentiles.

- Jesus's position in this debate reflects his views on holiness. Holiness was required to enter the Kingdom of God, according to the Gospel accounts. And therefore, one must love all others—everyone else, not just Jews, not just your neighbors, everyone—in order to imitate God's perfection.

Suggested Reading

Schiffman, *Texts and Traditions*, chapter 3, "Judaism in the Persian Period," pp. 65–70, 73–79.

VanderKam, *An Introduction to Early Judaism*, "The Elephantine Papyri," pp. 147–150.

Questions to Consider
1. What is the point of the story told in the Book of Tobit?

2. What is the significance of the temple to YHW at Elephantine?

Lecture

7   Alexander the Great's Impact on the Jews

In this lecture, our story starts in 336 B.C., when Philip II of Macedon was assassinated and his son Alexander became king of Macedonia and ruler of Greece. Two years later, Alexander launched an invasion of the Persian Empire; over the course of the next few years, Alexander fought and won three major battles against the Persian King Darius III. Alexander eventually became ruler of all of Persia, and he continued to push eastward across the Indus River Valley into India. In this lecture, we discuss the conquest of Alexander the Great and Alexander's impact on the Jews and Jewish tradition. We conclude by exploring possible parallels between the traditions surrounding Alexander the Great in Jewish eschatological thought and the mythology of Jesus.

Jewish Traditions about Alexander the Great
- During the course of Alexander the Great's march through the Persian Empire, he traveled to Egypt in 332 B.C. While there, he took two significant actions that would contribute to his legacy: He founded a new city on the coast, Alexandria, named after himself, and he visited an oracular shrine dedicated to the god Zeus Ammon in the Siwa Oasis. Of particular consequence is that when Alexander approached the shrine, he was greeted by the local priests as if he were a god.

- The Judeans were now under Alexander's rule. However, Greek historians do not mention Jerusalem or the Jews in connection with Alexander's conquest, which is not surprising because Judea was the home of an obscure people and an insignificant tribe. In fact, no contemporary Jewish sources refer to Alexander either.

- In order to reach Egypt from the north, Alexander would have traveled along the coast. It is unlikely that he would have taken the mountainous roads into the interior of the country, which would have led to Judea and Jerusalem.

The Judeans submitted peacefully to Alexander as he marched through Palestine on his way to Egypt.

- When Alexander took the coastal road to Egypt, he had to make arrangements to administer the country. It is significant that he maintained the religious and political privileges that the Jews had enjoyed under the Persians. Basically, he left the governing system intact and replaced the Persian officials and administrators with his own officials.

- In the centuries after the death of Alexander, when he became "the Great," the Jews sought to associate themselves with Alexander and his greatness. Jewish sources told of a supposed visit by Alexander to Judea and Jerusalem, and other traditions began to develop and circulate, as well.
    - Perhaps the best known of these stories is Daniel's vision, which is told in Daniel 8:1–27. In this passage, Daniel is shown a vision that involves a ram and a he-goat. The passage explicitly identifies the ram, which has two horns, with the king of Media and Persia—hence, the two horns. The he-goat, coming from the west, is Alexander the Great, who conquers the ram; in other words, Alexander conquers the Persian Empire.

    - Daniel's vision relates to the coming end of days, embedding Alexander in Jewish eschatological thought.

- Another celebrated legend involving the Jews and Alexander is preserved by the Jewish historian Flavius Josephus.
    - According to Josephus, in visiting Jerusalem, Alexander was greeted by the Jewish high priest, Jaddua, who presented the king with the Jewish community's capitulation; then, Alexander offered a sacrifice in the Jerusalem Temple.

    - In this story, not only did Alexander make a detour in order to meet with the Jews and go to Jerusalem, but when he saw the high priest and the name of God, he was so awed that he bowed down. Alexander, according to this legend, recognized the greatness of the God of Israel.

Alexander and the Samaritans
- What happened with the Samaritans under Alexander provides an interesting contrast with the legend of Alexander among the Jews. While the Jews submitted peacefully to Alexander, the Samaritans did not. At first, the Samaritan governor, Sanballat III, supported Alexander and was even given permission by him to build the Samaritan temple on Mount Gerizim. However, after Sanballat III died, the Samaritans, for reasons that are not clear, rebelled against Alexander and burned his governor alive.

- In punishment, Alexander destroyed the city of Samaria and banished the Samaritans from the city. The Samaritans went to live at the foot of Mount Gerizim, their sacred mountain. From that point on, the district of Samaria had two religious and political centers: the Samaritan, or Yahwist, population that was concentrated in the area of Mount Gerizim, and Samaria itself, which became a Greek city.

Alexander's Empire after His Death
- Alexander died in 323 B.C., and his death plunged his empire into a civil war that lasted for the next 20 years. Eventually, his empire was divided among various generals, the two most important being Seleucus and Ptolemy.

- Seleucus received most of Asia Minor, Syria, and Mesopotamia. This was known as the Seleucid kingdom. Ptolemy received Egypt, which became known as the Ptolemaic kingdom.

- Judea was located right between the Seleucids to the north and the Ptolemies to the south. During most of the 3rd century B.C., it was under the rule of the Ptolemies. During most of the 2nd century B.C., it was under the rule of the Seleucids.

Hellenization
- One of the challenges that Alexander's successors faced was to legitimize themselves as the heirs of Alexander in the eyes of the local populations. The problem here was that none of Alexander's

successors was actually related to Alexander. In antiquity, the law of succession was usually dynastic and proceeded through family ties.

- One way that these generals established their legitimacy as Alexander's successors was to imitate what Alexander had done. Specifically, they founded Greek cities, which they named after themselves. Each of these cities was a *polis* with Greek-style institutions, such as theaters for the performance of Greek plays, temples dedicated to Greek gods, council houses for Greek-style meetings, and *gymnasia* so that the youth could be educated in the Greek manner.

- The populations who lived in these cities grew loyal to the king because they benefited from the sophisticated Greek cultural and political institutions. The spreading of Greek culture in this way is called *Hellenization*, and it was an effective tool used throughout the realms ruled by Alexander's successors.

Parallels between Alexander and Jesus

- A number of possible parallels exist in the later traditions and legacies surrounding both Alexander the Great and Jesus Christ. These parallels have been explored by the scholar Ory Amitay in *From Alexander to Jesus*. In his book, Amitay examines the ways in which Alexander might have served as a model for the mythical Jesus. Importantly, Amitay focuses on the mythical Jesus rather than the historical Jesus—that is, the traditions that surrounded Jesus after his death.

- In the Greek and Roman world, it was common for royal families to trace their ancestry back to a hero or a god. In this case, Alexander's family traced its ancestry back to the Greek hero Heracles or Hercules. Amitay argues that Alexander lived his entire life in emulation, competition, and self-identification with Heracles. This established a basis for Alexander's transformation from human to divine, which was not a characteristic of the Greek world before then. This was a new feature introduced into Greek culture—the idea that the ruler becomes a god and is worshipped as one.

- In addition, Amitay points out that Alexander's legacy adopted a number of motifs from the mythology of Heracles. Not only do we see a divine ancestry going back to Heracles, but there are also other aspects of the mythology of Heracles that became features of traditions surrounding Alexander: the divine son, double paternity, a world mission on behalf of humanity, and divinization. Interestingly, these motifs are also a part of the myths associated with Jesus.

Prelude to the Messiah

- Alexander was already a key figure in Jewish eschatological thought, that is, Jewish thinking and expectations about what would happen at the end of days. In Jewish eschatological thought, Alexander is situated at the beginning of a new era that is perceived as the last stage of history before the end of days—the eschaton. In other words, Alexander was understood as a necessary step on the road to the advent of the messiah.

- We have already seen that Alexander played a key role in the most influential piece of apocalyptic literature produced by Second Temple–period Judaism: the Book of Daniel. According to this book, Daniel stands in the royal court of three successive kingdoms: Babylon, Media, and Persia.

- Daniel looks into the future and sees the progress of human history in a series of distinct visions presented as a succession of kingdoms. The fourth and last kingdom is Macedonia; this kingdom—significantly—is to be followed by God's kingdom. The perception of Alexander as the instigator of the last stage in history before the messianic kingdom would become a staple in Jewish traditions about the end of days.

- One of the central questions posed by Amitay is how a monotheistic religion led to mythology about the son of God.

Amitay proposes that Alexander is the key figure here. Amitay argues that Alexander's historical role as the paragon of divinization helped prepare the way for the acceptance by Jews of the principle of the divine son. Alexander was a flesh-and-blood person who broke the barrier between humanity and the divine. Another well-known parallel between Alexander and Jesus is that both died at the age of 33.

- Amitay notes that Alexander was a bridge between the worlds of monotheism and polytheism. He concludes, "Alexander and Jesus were close neighbors in the boiling matrix of God's heroes and demons which characterized the religious life of later antiquity."

Suggested Reading
Schiffman, *Texts and Traditions*, chapter 4, "The Hellenistic Age," pp. 121–125, 130–134.

Questions to Consider
1. How did Alexander the Great's conquest affect the Jews in the short term and in the long term?

2. In what ways might Alexander have served as a model for the mythical Jesus?

Lecture

8   Jews and Greek Rule: The Heliodorus Affair

Alexander the Great's death in 323 B.C. was followed by a 20-year civil war over succession. Eventually, the empire was divided up among various generals. Seleucus took the area to the north, and Ptolemy took Egypt, to the south. In this lecture, we discuss the establishment of the Ptolemaic and Seleucid kingdoms, explore the consequences of the "Heliodorus affair," and examine the efforts of the high priest Jason to transform Jerusalem into a Greek *polis* called Antioch.

Judea under the Ptolemies and Seleucids

- Flavius Josephus reports that Ptolemy I took Jerusalem through deception in the year 301 B.C. He entered the city under the pretense of offering a sacrifice in the temple, knowing that the unsuspecting Jews would not fight on the Sabbath. Jerusalem and Judea remained under the rule of the Ptolemies until 198 B.C., when the Seleucid king Antiochus III took Jerusalem after a long siege. Antiochus III's victory is described in Daniel 11:14–15, which mentions Jerusalem as a "well-fortified city."

- Under both the Ptolemies and the Seleucids, administrative and political changes were made throughout the territories. Jerusalem and Judea now belonged to a province called Syria. The provinces, including Syria, were headed by a civil and military administrator called, in Greek, a *strategos*. Each province was subdivided into smaller units; the *toparchy* was a territory that centered on a city.

- Jerusalem and Judea were administered differently from the rest of the province of Syria. Under Greek rule, the Jews of Judea constituted a self-governing people. The Ptolemies and Seleucids followed the precedent set by the Persians and Alexander the Great and allowed the Jews to govern themselves autonomously and to live according to the laws in the five books of Moses.

- Judea was governed by a council of prominent priests and elders, which was called the *gerusia*, headed by the high priest. In other words, the government in Judea was a theocracy. Under the Seleucids, the Jews of Judea were classified as an *ethnos*. Therefore, a Jew—or, in Greek, Ioudaios—was not just a person of the Jewish religion but a person of Judean parentage whose place of origin was legally Judea.

- Such an individual was obliged to worship the God of Israel because the laws of the Torah were the laws of the land. In fact, in his charter, Antiochus III proclaimed, "All members of this ethnos shall be governed in accordance with their ancestral laws," meaning the five books of Moses.

- In other words, following the tradition established by the Persians, the Torah had the status of royal law in Judea. This key fact sets us up for understanding the series of events known as the Heliodorus affair.

The Heliodorus Affair

- The historical episode known as the Heliodorus affair was a key turning point in the history of the Jews in Judea. It is an episode that reflects internal struggles for power and factional conflicts between the powerful, elite families of Jerusalem.

- The Heliodorus affair began when the authority of the high priest Onias III was challenged by a certain man named Simon, who had been appointed captain of the temple by the Seleucid king. Simon accused Onias III of hoarding large sums of money in the Jerusalem Temple, meaning that the high priest was not declaring this money to the king.

- King Seleucus IV then sent his finance minister, Heliodorus, to Jerusalem. But when Heliodorus arrived in Jerusalem, Onias III told him that the money in the temple was the savings of widows and orphans and, therefore, could not be confiscated. Heliodorus then left Jerusalem. Onias III departed for Antioch to meet with Seleucus IV and clear his name.

- But Onias III never got the chance to argue his case before Seleucus IV because the king was assassinated by Heliodorus; then, Heliodorus was driven out by Seleucus's brother, Antiochus IV. Antiochus IV ruled the Seleucid kingdom from 175 to 164 B.C.

Jerusalem as a *Polis*

- While Onias III was in Antioch, seeking a hearing with the Seleucid king, his brother Jason served for him as high priest in the Jerusalem Temple. When Antiochus IV became king, Jason moved to secure the high priesthood for himself, offering the king 360 talents of silver and, from another source of revenue, 80 talents. And then Jason made another request—specifically, to turn Jerusalem into a Greek city.

- The most significant consequence of Jason's action was that Jerusalem became a *polis*, which meant that Greek law replaced Jewish law as the law of the land. The author of 2 Maccabees describes the actions of Jason: "He set aside the royal ordinances especially favoring the Jews and abrogating the lawful ways of living. He introduced new customs contrary to the law, for he willingly established a *gymnasium* right under the citadel, and he made the finest of the young men wear the Greek hat."

- Jerusalem now possessed all the characteristic features of a Greek city, with Greek law as the law of the land and Greek institutions established in the city. The author of 2 Maccabees describes this transformation, noting that "the cultivation of Greek fashions and the coming in of foreign customs" rose to such a pitch that the priests "were no longer earnest about the services of the altar."

- It is important to note here that the initiatives for the transformation of Jerusalem into a Greek *polis* came from within the Jewish community itself. This was not imposed on the Jews by the Greek king.

- Furthermore, there is no reference in 2 Maccabees to any Jewish opposition to Jason's actions. None of the texts we have accuse Jason of altering the cult in the Jerusalem Temple or prohibiting the normal practices of Judaism. Thus, even though Jewish law was no longer the law of the land, the Jews were still free to worship the God of Israel in the Jerusalem Temple and to live according to the Torah. Jason's high priesthood lasted from 175 to 172 B.C.—a defining moment in the history of the Jews in Judea.

Tax Farming

- Under the Ptolemies, taxes were collected through a system of *tax farming*. Just like the office of the priest, the office of tax collector could be bought and sold. Thus, the system of tax farming led to cooperation between the kings and the wealthiest families, because only the wealthiest families could bid on the office. But the most significant consequence of tax farming was that it created an enormous burden on the people—especially on the poor.

- Of course, the point of being a tax collector was to enrich oneself. Tax collectors—or tax farmers—lined their pockets by collecting more and more taxes, above and beyond the amount that they were permitted. In fact, the phrase "tax collectors and sinners" occurs nine times in the New Testament.

- It was not just the Greek successors of Alexander the Great who used a system of tax farming; in fact, from the time of the republic, the Romans did so, as well. Taxes were collected by men called *publicani*—public contractors who supplied the Roman army, collected port duties, and oversaw public building projects. By the 2nd and 1st centuries B.C., most of Rome's taxes came from the provinces.

- In the Roman world, the right to collect taxes in different provinces or regions was auctioned to the highest bidder, just as it had been in the Greek world. Individual *publicani* were usually members of the elite equestrian class; they frequently formed companies in order to bid on a large scale. Membership in a company of *publicani* was open only to Roman citizens.

- In order to collect the taxes in the provinces, the *publicani* employed local representatives. Luke 19:2 probably refers to one of these representatives: "A man was there named Zacchaeus. He was a chief tax collector and was rich."

- Augustus replaced tax farming with direct taxation by requiring each province to pay a wealth tax of about 1 percent and a flat poll tax on each adult. This reform required regular census taking to evaluate the taxable number of people and their income or wealth status. Nevertheless, the custom of tax farming continued, together with the abuses associated with it, because provincial governors under the Romans continued to employ private tax farmers to collect revenues.

- Provincial governors and tax collectors enriched themselves by collecting more than the official rate. Authors of the New Testament protested; in Luke 3:12–13, we read: "Even tax collectors came to be baptized. And they asked him 'Master, what should we do?' He said to them, 'Collect no more than the amount prescribed for you.'"

- In addition, provincial governors and tax collectors bought up grain at a low rate at harvest time, which they sold at inflated rates in times of shortage. They also lent money to desperate provincials at usurious rates of 4 percent or more per month. The tax collectors mentioned in the Gospel accounts—in Mark, Matthew, and Luke—generally were the local provincial agents who actually collected the taxes, including Matthew the apostle.

Suggested Reading

Goldenberg, *The Origins of Judaism*, chapter 4, "Crisis and a New Beginning."

Schiffman, *Texts and Traditions*, chapter 4, "The Hellenistic Age," pp. 147–150.

Questions to Consider

1. What was the Heliodorus affair, and what were its consequences?

2. Who were the tax collectors mentioned in the Gospel accounts?

Lecture 9

Desolating Sacrilege and the Maccabean Revolt

In 167 B.C., Antiochus IV decreed "that all should be one people and that all should give up their particular customs." The Jerusalem Temple was rededicated to the worship of the Greek god Zeus, and the practice of Judaism was now outlawed—a crime punishable by death. Antiochus IV's edict sparked the outbreak of a Jewish revolt, led by the Maccabees. In this lecture, we cover the turbulent period in Judea before and during the Maccabean Revolt. We conclude by considering the Book of Daniel, which was written around the time of the revolt, and examine the term "desolating sacrilege," which occurs in Daniel and is repeated in Jesus's prophesies about the destruction of the Temple of Jerusalem.

The Decree of Antiochus IV

- In 172 B.C., Jason sent Menelaus to Antiochus IV to make a payment in order to maintain his position as high priest in the Temple of Jerusalem. However, Menelaus betrayed Jason and secured the high priesthood for himself, outbidding Jason by 300 talents of silver. Menelaus was from a priestly family, but he was not from the Zadokite line—the family that had traditionally held the high priesthood in the Jerusalem Temple. The Zadokites lost control of the high priesthood, and Jason was driven out of Jerusalem.

- According to 1 Maccabees, Antiochus IV issued a decree to all his people, in which he directed them to:

    follow customs strange to the land, to forbid burnt offerings and sacrifices and drink offerings in the sanctuary, to profane Sabbaths and festivals, to defile the sanctuary and the priests, to build altars and sacred precincts for idols, to sacrifice swine and other unclean animals, and to leave their sons uncircumcised. They were to make themselves abominable by everything unclean and profane so that they would forget the law and change all the ordinances. Whoever does not obey the command of the King shall die.

- As a result of Antiochus IV's decree, the Temple of Jerusalem was rededicated to the worship of the Greek Olympian god Zeus, and the Samaritan temple on Mount Gerizim was rededicated to Zeus Hellenios. Judaism was outlawed—a crime punishable by death.

The Maccabean Revolt

- Antiochus IV's edict sparked the outbreak of a Jewish revolt, led by members of a family called the Hasmoneans. The revolt began when Mattathias, patriarch of the Hasmonean clan, executed a king's officer, tore down an altar, and fled with his sons to the hills. Recruits soon joined the rebels, who were led by one of Mattathias's sons, Judah, also called Maccabee, meaning "The Hammer."

- Judah and his companions secretly entered the villages, summoned their kinsmen, and enlisted those who had continued in the Jewish faith. They gathered about 6,000 men. The first phase of the Maccabean Revolt was actually a bloody civil war, in which the Hasmoneans used terrorist tactics and armed warfare against their opponents.

- According to 1 Maccabees, "He, Judah, searched out and pursued the lawless. He, Judah, burned those who troubled his people. Lawless men shrank back for fear of him. All the evildoers were confounded, and deliverance prospered by his hand. He went through the cities of Judah. He destroyed the ungodly out of the land. Thus he turned away wrath from Israel."

- The author of 1 Maccabees describes the Jews who did not observe Jewish law as "lawless." These are the people who were persecuted and wiped out by Judah and his followers. At the same time as this civil war within Judaism, the Hasmoneans also conducted guerrilla warfare against the Seleucids and were able to defeat the Seleucids in several crucial battles.

The Hanukkah menorah recalls the sacred candelabrum that was in the Jerusalem Temple and, by way of extension, the Jerusalem Temple itself.

The Decree of Antiochus V

- In 164 B.C., Antiochus IV died and was succeeded to the throne by his son Antiochus V. Antiochus V, still a young boy, issued an edict that reversed his father's decree. He wrote: "We have heard that the Jews do not consent to our father's change to Greek customs but prefer their own way of living and ask that their customs be allowed them. Accordingly, since we choose that this nation should also be free from disturbance, our decision is that their temple be restored to them and that they live according to the customs of their ancestors."

- Antiochus V's decree allowed the Jews to return to the practice of Judaism and to live according to the laws of the God of Israel, without fear of persecution or death. Furthermore, Antiochus V returned the Temple of Jerusalem to the Jews, allowing them to rededicate it to the worship of the God of Israel.

- The Temple of Jerusalem was ritually purified, and the Jewish sacrificial cult was restored there. This event took place on the 25th day of the Jewish month of Kislev, which is approximately the middle of December, in the year 164 B.C. This occasion became the basis for the Jewish festival later known as Hanukkah.

The Book of Daniel and the "Desolating Sacrilege"

- These events had a deep impact on the Jews of Judea and are reflected in contemporary literature, including the Book of Daniel, one of the major works of this turbulent period in Jewish history. For example, in Daniel 9:26–27, we read, "Desolations are decreed. He, Antiochus IV, shall make a strong covenant with many."

- The "many" here refers to Hellenized Jews. Indeed, there were a great many Jews in Jerusalem who were eager to adopt Greek culture. These were the Hellenized Jews who were opposed by the Hasmoneans and condemned by the author of 1 Maccabees. These Hellenized Jews were even members of the priestly families.

- There are repeated references in Daniel to an abomination of desolation, a desolating sacrilege, or a transgression. The Hebrew term is *shikkutz shomem*. The desolating sacrilege is mentioned not only in Daniel but also in 1 Maccabees 54: "Now on the 15th day of Kislev, in the 145th year, they erected a desolating sacrilege on the altar of burnt offering."

- The "desolating sacrilege" in the books of Daniel and 1 Maccabees seems to refer to an altar to Zeus that was erected by Antiochus IV in the Temple of Jerusalem. Sources indicate that the cult of Zeus in the Jerusalem Temple would have been accompanied by many customs that not only were foreign to Judaism but would have been considered abominations because they transgressed Jewish law—for example, the offering and consumption of pork or sacred prostitution.

- According to the Gospel accounts, Jesus foretold the destruction of the Temple of Jerusalem and described signs of the end of days. For example, Matthew 24:15–16 says, "So when you see the desolating sacrilege standing in the holy place, as was spoken of by the prophet Daniel, let the reader understand. Then those in Judea must flee to the mountains." Notice the explicit reference to Daniel's prediction.

- Mark 13:14 says, "But when you see the desolating sacrilege, set up where it ought not to be. Let the reader understand. Then those in Judea must flee to the mountains." There is a similar passage in Luke 21.

- The prophecy that Jesus reportedly makes in the Gospel accounts draws explicitly on the Book of Daniel. It implies that the prophecy of the "desolating sacrilege" in Daniel 9:27 is about to be fulfilled. In other words, the authors here draw on the prophecies in the Book of Daniel in setting up the arrival of the end of days.

- In Daniel, the "desolating sacrilege" probably refers to an altar that Antiochus IV set up to Zeus in the Temple of Jerusalem. But what does the term mean in the New Testament? It is difficult to answer this question, because the answer depends on the date of the composition of the Gospel accounts—specifically, whether they were written before or after 70 A.D.
    - Notice a crucial difference in the passages of Mark and Matthew. Mark says, "But when you see the desolating sacrilege, set up where it ought not to be." Matthews says, "So when you see the desolating sacrilege standing in the holy place."

    - Mark is generally thought by scholars to be the earliest of the canonical Gospels, written either shortly before 70 A.D. or soon afterward, whereas Matthew is usually dated by scholars somewhere around 80 to 90 A.D. Thus, the writers of these two Gospels did not necessarily understand the "desolating sacrilege" to be the same phenomenon. Their contexts were different because they wrote at different times.

- The author of the Gospel of Mark might have thought that the desolating sacrilege was a statue that the Romans would set up in the temple in the future—just as the Roman emperor Caligula had intended to do several decades earlier, around 40 A.D. The author of the Gospel of Matthew, in contrast, might have thought that the desolating sacrilege was the Roman general Titus standing in the temple in 70 A.D.

Suggested Reading

Nickelsburg, *Jewish Literature between the Bible and the Mishnah*, chapter 3, "Reform—Repression—Revolt," pp. 67–69, 77–83.

VanderKam, *An Introduction to Early Judaism*, chapter 1, "The Time of the Second Temple," pp. 12–24.

Questions to Consider

1. What were the consequences of the edict issued by Antiochus IV Epiphanes?

2. What is the "desolating sacrilege" of the Book of Daniel and the Gospel accounts?

Lecture

10 Apocalyptic Works and the "Son of Man"

Literary works composed in the aftermath of the Maccabean Revolt were an expression of the Jews' reactions to events at this time. In this lecture, we examine historical works and apocalyptic literature, including 1 Maccabees, 2 Maccabees, and the books of Daniel and Enoch. We conclude by discussing the possible meanings of the term "son of man" in the New Testament in general and the Gospels in particular.

1 and 2 Maccabees

- The books of 1 and 2 Maccabees are apocryphal works, which means that they are included in the Catholic Bible but not in the Hebrew Bible or Protestant Bible. The book 1 Maccabees was written in Hebrew around 100 B.C.; it is an important historical source for events in Judea in the 2nd century B.C.

- The book 2 Maccabees tells us more about itself than most ancient writings. The author of 2 Maccabees apparently came from Alexandria in Egypt. He calls his book, written in Greek, a summary of a lost five-volume work by a certain Jason of Cyrene. This book is our only source of information for significant events in Jerusalem during the 180s and 170s B.C.—especially relating to the Heliodorus affair.

- The book 2 Maccabees is an example of what is called *pathetic historiography*. In this term, the word *pathetic* is derived from the Greek *pathos*, meaning "emotion." The author of 2 Maccabees attempts to evoke the emotions of the readers through what he is writing.

Apocalyptic Literature

- The word *apocalyptic* comes from the Greek *apokalypsis*, which means "to unveil." Apocalyptic literature deals with the revelation of secret knowledge. Examples of apocalyptic works include

Lecture 10—Apocalyptic Works and the "Son of Man"

Apocalyptic literature, such as the Book of Revelation, is associated with the unveiling of secret knowledge; an expectation of the end of days may also be bound up with apocalyptic views.

Daniel, Enoch, Jubilees, 4 Ezra, and in the New Testament, the Book of Revelation.

- The main characteristics of apocalyptic literature are the following:
  - Pseudonymity, or false names. In apocalyptic literature, visions are attributed to noted figures from the past; these figures make the secrets of history known to believers.

  - Numerical symbolism. Numbers always have a symbolic value in apocalyptic literature. For example, the number 4 usually denotes totality. Other key numbers are 7 and 12.

  - Secret language. Use of a secret language in apocalyptic literature means that names from the past are often used to denote contemporary rulers and lands. A well-known example of this is in the Book of Revelation, where Babylon denotes Rome. Another use of secret language is that animals often represent specific individuals.

  - Doctrine of angels. For example, Daniel mentions the angels Gabriel and Michael; they belong to the group of four or seven archangels mentioned in other apocalyptic works.

  - Division of history into periods. In apocalyptic literature, history is typically divided into a series of periods, after which comes the time of salvation. For example, in Daniel 7, we read: "These great beasts, four in number, are four kings who shall arise out of the earth. The fourth beast shall be a fourth kingdom on the earth, which shall be different from all the other kingdoms."

  - Time of salvation. In apocalyptic literature, the "world to come" will emerge after the downfall of this world. According to this expectation, which is expressed in visions, the coming messiah becomes increasingly significant.

The Book of Daniel

- Apocalyptic literature became especially prominent around 165 B.C.—at the time of the Maccabean Revolt. This is not surprising, because apocalyptic movements and expectations usually emerge in times of oppression and persecution.

- The aim of apocalyptic literature is to give encouragement to the oppressed by stressing that all powers, even the greatest world empires, will not last and that eventually the Kingdom of God—the time of salvation—will come.

- The Book of Daniel is by far the most significant work from the time of the Maccabean Revolt. From a literary point of view, the work consists of a narrative section, chapters 1–6, followed by an apocalyptic section, chapters 7–12. Part of the Book of Daniel is in Hebrew, and part is in Aramaic. Despite the book's complexity, most scholars believe that it is a literary unity. The Book of Daniel had a tremendous influence on Jewish and, later, Christian beliefs and expectations.

Flood Stories

- In addition to the Book of Daniel, there is another corpus of apocalyptic literature that is equally important but not as well known: Enochic literature. Enochic literature refers to Jewish apocalyptic works centering on Enoch, the grandfather of Noah. Works associated with Enoch are, by extension, connected to stories of the flood.

- Flood stories have a long history in the ancient Near East. The oldest version of the flood story that we have is Sumerian and dates to the 3rd millennium B.C. About 1800 B.C., an author compiled earlier stories, including a flood story, into a great work called the Epic of Gilgamesh. Gilgamesh was a king of the Sumerian city of Uruk sometime around 2700–2500 B.C.
  - The hero of this story is named Utnapishtim. Utnapishtim tells Gilgamesh that the god Ea instructed him to build a ship: "These are the measurements of the bark as you shall

build her. Let her beam equal her width. Let her deck be roofed like the vault that covers the abyss. Then take up into the boat the seed of all living creatures."

- o Notice that the characters in this story, in anticipation of the flood, build a large boat and take the seeds of all living creatures onto it.

- In both the Gilgamesh epic and 1 Enoch, the revelation of secret knowledge is associated with a key figure. In Gilgamesh, we read: "Utnapishtim said to him, 'I will reveal to thee, Gilgamesh, a hidden matter, and a secret of the gods I will tell thee.'" In 1 Enoch, we read: "And after that, my grandfather Enoch gave me the teaching of all the secrets in the Book of Parables, which had been given to him."

Enochic Literature
- If we look back at Genesis, we find that Enoch was not only the grandfather of Noah but also the seventh forefather from Adam. According to Genesis: "Thus all the days of Enoch were 365 years. Enoch walked with God. Then he was no more, because God took him." The number of years Enoch lived, of course, recalls the number of days in a calendar year. In fact, among the mysteries that supposedly were revealed to Enoch in later traditions were secrets about time and the solar calendar.

- In the late Second Temple period and later, a great deal of speculation arose about what had happened to Enoch. This speculation resulted in a vast corpus of writing called Enochic literature—the various books of Enoch. In this literature, Enoch became a prototype of a righteous man who lived in a righteous age—that is, in the age before the flood. At some point, Enochic literature transformed Enoch into a heavenly priest and a divine angel, through whom God's secrets, especially the secrets of time, were revealed to humans.

- Eventually, Enochic literature transformed Enoch into a figure called Metatron—the most powerful angel in heaven. Metatron is described as a second Yahweh.

The "Son of Man"
- The Hebrew term for "son of man" is *ben adam*; it can refer simply to humans versus the divine. If we look at other examples, however, "son of man" does not always mean just a human being.
    - For example, in Daniel 7:13, we read: "As I watched in the night visions, I saw one like a son of man coming with the clouds of heaven. And he came to the ancient one and was presented before him." In this passage, "the ancient one" is God, who is seated on his throne in heaven, surrounded by angels. Here, "son of man" refers to an angel who looks human—likely Michael.

    - According to Daniel 7:14, the son of man was given "eternal dominion over all peoples and nations." We see something similar in the Enochic traditions. For example, in 1 Enoch, the son of man seems to be an angelic figure with a human appearance who is identified as Enoch himself. Similar to what we see in Daniel, we have a juxtaposition between the ancient one—God—and a son of man—an angelic figure with a human appearance.

- We also see the term *son of man* in the New Testament, where depending on the context, it can take on different meanings. *Son of man* can either mean a simple human, or the term can draw on the meaning used in the apocalyptic sections of Daniel.
    - In the Gospel accounts, the phrase *son of man* occurs with the definite article: "the son of man." For example, in Matthew 24:30–31, we read: "Then the sign of the Son of Man will appear in heaven. And then all the tribes of the earth will mourn, and they will see the Son of Man coming on the clouds of heaven with power and great glory."

- - Matthew 24:37–39 says, "For as the days of Noah were, so will be the coming of the Son of Man. For as in those days before the flood, they were eating and drinking, marrying and giving in marriage, until the day Noah entered the ark, and they knew nothing until the flood came and swept them away. So too will be the coming of the Son of Man."

  - In Matthew 25:31–32, we read, "When the Son of Man comes in his glory and all the angels with him, then he will sit on the throne of his glory. All the nations will be gathered before him. And he will separate people one from another, as a shepherd separates the sheep from the goats."

- In these above passages in the Gospel accounts, the son of man becomes a judge at the end of days, whereas in Daniel 7, the son of man appears after the judgment. In order to understand the references in the New Testament to the son of man, it is important to understand the meaning of the term in earlier Jewish traditions, including Jewish apocalyptic literature.

Suggested Reading

Nickelsburg, *Ancient Judaism and Christian Origins*, chapter 5, "Eschatology," pp. 120–134.

Schiffman, *Texts and Traditions*, chapter 4, "The Hellenistic Age," pp. 151–169.

Questions to Consider

1. What are the characteristics of apocalyptic literature, and what is the purpose of this literature?

2. What is Enochic literature?

Lecture

11   Jesus's Jewish Lineage

In 164 B.C., Antiochus V rescinded his father's edict, and once again, the Jews were allowed to practice their religion without persecution and rededicate the Temple of Jerusalem. In that same year, the Maccabees renewed their conflict with the Seleucids, with the goal of gaining independence from Greek rule. In this lecture, the establishment and expansion of the Hasmonean, or Maccabean, kingdom provide the context for understanding the birth narratives of Jesus in the Gospels of Matthew and Luke.

Independence from Seleucid Rule

- For a number of years after 164 B.C., battles continued between the Hasmoneans, or Maccabees, and the Seleucids. In 160 B.C., Judah was killed in battle and was succeeded as leader by his brother Jonathan. In 152 B.C., Jonathan managed to become ruler of Judea by aligning himself with a contestant to the Seleucid throne. In addition to granting Jonathan the right to rule over the Jews, the Seleucid king also made him high priest.

- This move was opposed by many Jews because Jonathan, although of priestly descent, was not a member of the Zadokites. Moreover, high priests, according to biblical Jewish law, were not supposed to have blood on their hands, and Jonathan had been a leader of the revolt and had fought many battles.

- Jonathan ruled until his death in 142 B.C., when he was succeeded by his brother Simon, the youngest and last of the Maccabean brothers. Under Simon, the Jews gained complete independence from Seleucid rule; Simon ruled until his death in 134 B.C.

Judaization

- Simon was succeeded as ruler by his son John Hyrcanus I, who expanded his realm through military conquest, adding Samaria to the north of Judea, Idumea to the south, and territories in Transjordan.

- During the course of these conquests, John Hyrcanus I forced the populations to convert to Judaism. Flavius Josephus writes, "He, John Hyrcanus, permitted them to remain in their country so long as they had themselves circumcised and were willing to observe the laws of the Jews." One of the people forcibly converted to Judaism at this time was the grandfather of King Herod the Great.

- Today, according to Jewish tradition, Jews are not allowed to forcibly convert others to Judaism. In fact, Jews try to discourage people who want to convert to Judaism. In this period in history, however, no such prohibition existed. In fact, we have evidence that, in antiquity, Jews proselytized widely.

- This forced conversion may have been a kind of Jewish parallel to Hellenization. Greek successors of Alexander carried out a policy of Hellenization within their kingdoms—that is, they spread Greek culture as a means of homogenizing the diverse populations under their rule. The Hasmonean kings may have been using Judaism in a similar manner, to spread Jewish culture—a process of Judaization versus Hellenization.

Rebellion against Alexander Jannaeus

- John Hyrcanus I ruled until his death in 104 B.C. and was succeeded by his son Aristobulus I. Aristobulus I ruled only briefly, until his death of an illness in 103 B.C. He was survived by his widow, Salome Alexandra; she then married her husband's brother, Alexander Jannaeus, who ruled until 76 B.C.

- This kind of union, called *levirate marriage*, is mandated by biblical law. Similar laws go back to the tribal system in Israelite society, which was concerned with preserving the bloodlines of the family. Although biblical law mandates levirate marriage, however, marrying his brother's widow actually showed

Alexander Jannaeus's disregard for Jewish law—because another biblical law prohibits high priests from marrying widows.

- Jannaeus was cruel and arrogant, and his reign aroused enormous opposition. In about 90 B.C., during Sukkot, the Feast of Tabernacles, which was one of the pilgrimage holidays to the Temple of Jerusalem, Alexander Jannaeus deliberately went against prescribed ritual by pouring holy water on the ground instead of on the altar.

- Some years after, an open rebellion broke out against Alexander Jannaeus. During the course of this civil war, Jannaeus's opponents called on the Seleucid king Demetrius III for help. Demetrius III invaded and defeated Alexander Jannaeus in a battle—at which point, however, the Jewish rebels apparently had second thoughts and decided that they preferred a bad Hasmonean king to a Seleucid.

The "Seekers of Smooth Things"

- The civil war against Alexander Jannaeus seems to be echoed in one of the Dead Sea Scrolls, called the Pesher Nahum, or the Commentary on Nahum. This genre of literature, *pesher*, is a commentary on a biblical book. Typically in these works, the author cites and interprets the relevant passage in a biblical book.

- The Pesher Nahum reads, "This concerns Demetrius King of Greece, who sought on the counsel of those who seek smooth things to enter Jerusalem. But God did not permit the city to be delivered into the hands of the kings of Greece from the time of Antiochus until the coming out of the rulers of the Kittim." The passage goes on: "Interpreted, this concerns the furious young lion who executes revenge on those who seek smooth things."

- The expression "seekers of smooth things" is an example of a derogatory pun. The "seekers of smooth things" in Hebrew is *dorshei hachalakot*. The pun is *dorshei hahalachot*, which means "seekers of the law." The author of Pesher Nahum is mocking the group by calling them not the seekers of the law but the seekers of smooth things—those who take the easy way out. In fact, "seekers of smooth things" is a name that the author of this scroll gave to an opposing group—the Pharisees.

Connection between Jesus and David

- Our review of the various rulers of the Hasmonean kingdom sets us up for discussing the birth narratives in the Gospels of Matthew and Luke. Matthew and Luke are the only two of the four canonical Gospels that contain birth narratives. If we read them side by side, we see that the birth narratives in these two Gospels differ quite a bit.

- Matthew opens with "an account of the genealogy of Jesus the Messiah, the son of David." Notice that this genealogy goes directly from Jesus to David. Matthew then continues with the divine conception, Jesus's birth in Bethlehem, the visit of the three Magi, and the flight to Egypt. Then, we are introduced to John the Baptist.

- In contrast, Luke has a prologue dedicated to Theophilus, which in Greek means "lover of God." Then, Luke foretells the birth of John the Baptist, followed by the birth of Jesus: "In the sixth month, the angel Gabriel was sent by God to a town in Galilee called Nazareth to a virgin engaged to a man whose name was Joseph of the house of David." Also in Luke, we read, "Joseph also went from the town of Nazareth in Galilee to Judea to the City of David called Bethlehem because he was descended from the house and family of David." Notice the repeated emphasis here on David and the concern to connect Jesus with David.

- In contrast, the Gospels of Mark and John have no birth narratives. Instead, they open with the ministry of John the Baptist. We are first introduced to Jesus as an adult being baptized.

The narratives of Jesus's birth in the Gospels of Matthew and Luke connect Jesus with King David to fulfill expectations that the coming messiah would be descended from David.

- The authors of the Gospels of Matthew and Luke clearly went to great lengths to establish Jesus's descent from David. This goes back to biblical Jewish traditions—specifically, several passages in the Hebrew Bible. Consider, for example, 2 Samuel 7:1–29: "Moreover, the Lord declares to you that the Lord will make you a house. When your days are fulfilled and you lie down with your ancestors, I will raise up your offspring after you who shall come forth from your body and I will establish his kingdom. David says, for you O Lord God have spoken. And with your blessing, shall the house of your servant be blessed forever."

- By the 1st century B.C., the late Second Temple period, many Jews had come to anticipate the arrival of one or more messianic figures. These messianic figures were eschatological redeemers, who would come at the end of days, sent by God to reign over a restored Kingdom of Israel. This restored kingdom was frequently associated with David.

- It is important to realize that, at least among Jews in this period, these traditions always conceived of the messiahs as human beings, even if they may have had supernatural qualities. They were agents of God but not saviors in the Christian sense of the word.

- The assumption that Jesus must be descended from David in order to be the legitimate messiah underlies the birth narratives in Matthew and Luke. These Gospel authors went to great lengths to establish Jesus's descent from David because they took for granted the principle that to be the legitimate messiah, Jesus must be descended from David.

- In order to establish Jesus's descent from David, the Gospel authors had to connect Jesus with Bethlehem, which is located in Judea near Jerusalem. Bethlehem was David's hometown and the place where David was crowned king of Israel. The only problem was that Jesus was from Nazareth in Galilee.

- Jesus's origin in Galilee meant that his descent from David was questionable. Further, his Jewish descent would have been questionable, as well. In fact, Galilee had been Judaized by the Hasmoneans only a century before Jesus's birth. Therefore, by Jesus's time, the population of Galilee included non-Jews who had been Judaized, or forcibly converted to Judaism, by the Hasmoneans a century earlier, as well as descendants of Judean colonists.

- Matthew and Luke take great pains to insert birth narratives into their accounts that not only established Jesus as coming from Judea originally but also established his lineage going back to David, in order to bolster the claim that he was, in fact, a legitimate messiah.

Suggested Reading

Goldenberg, *The Origins of Judaism*, chapter 5, "The First Kingdom of Judaea."

VanderKam, *An Introduction to Early Judaism*, "The Hasmonean State," pp. 24–32.

Questions to Consider

1. How did the Hasmonean kings deal with the non-Jewish populations of newly conquered territories, and what was the consequence of their policy?

2. Who are the "seekers of smooth things" mentioned in some of the Dead Sea Scrolls?

Lecture

12 Was Jesus a Pharisee?

In this lecture, we discuss the emergence of the major Jewish sects in the late Second Temple period, specifically the Sadducees and the Pharisees. We compare and contrast the beliefs of these two sects with regard to resurrection of the dead, immortality of the soul, and free will and conclude by considering whether Jesus was a Pharisee.

Jewish Sects
- During the Hasmonean period, various Jewish factions or groups came into being in Judea. Josephus calls these groups *hairesis*, which is Greek for "heresies." The Latin word is *secta*, which means "sects" or "philosophies." Today's negative connotation of these terms comes out of Christianity, not early Judaism. In fact, in their original usage, the Latin *secta* and the Greek *hairesis* were simply neutral terms meaning a school of thought.

- Josephus specifically mentions three sects that developed among the Jews: the Pharisees, the Sadducees, and the particularly saintly Essenes. Although there is no scholarly agreement about the background against which these sects first developed, generally, scholars think that they originated and crystallized by the mid–2nd century B.C. In other words, these sects developed against the background of the Heliodorus affair and the Maccabean Revolt.

- The Sadducees originated from the Zadokites, who controlled the priesthood in the Temple of Jerusalem until the Heliodorus affair. At the point when the Zadokites lost control of the high priesthood in the Temple, the Zadokite line then split into at least three branches.

- One branch of this family was called the Oniads, named after Onias III, Onias IV, and their descendants. Sometime around the middle of the 2nd century B.C., Onias IV left Judea and went to

Egypt, where he established a temple dedicated to the God of Israel at a site called Leontopolis. The Oniads officiated as the priests in this temple until the temple was closed by the Emperor Vespasian in 73 A.D.

- Another branch of the Zadokites was central in the formation of the Essene sect. A third branch of the Zadokite family, the Sadducees, remained in Jerusalem, forming an alliance with the Hasmoneans and becoming an integral part of Jewish society for the next two centuries.

The Sadducees

- The information we have about the Sadducees actually comes from sources that were hostile to them. These sources include Josephus, who was a Pharisee. The New Testament and rabbinic literature are also associated with the Pharisees.

- The Sadducees were members of the priestly class and the aristocracy—wealthy members of Judean society consisting mostly of the Jerusalem elite. Not surprisingly, the Sadducees wanted to maintain the status quo. They were concerned with preserving political and social stability in order to secure and retain their own economic interests. What's more, they favored a policy of cooperation with foreign rulers.

- In addition to being politically conservative, the Sadducees were also religiously conservative. They recognized only the written tradition as holy scripture. In contrast to the Pharisees, the Sadducees rejected the principle of oral law—meaning an oral tradition that made new adaptations or interpretations of the written law possible.

- For example, while the Pharisees advocated the idea of a physical resurrection of the dead, the Sadducees rejected it because it had no explicit basis in the written law.

The Pharisees

- The name *Pharisees* may have derived from the Hebrew word *parash*, which means "to separate." They may have sought to separate themselves from the dominant priestly class or from those they considered to be lax in the observance of biblical purity laws. Issues of ritual purity and impurity were important to the Pharisees, who held themselves to much higher standards than most other Jews (except for the Essenes, who considered the Pharisees lax).

- The Pharisees usually referred to themselves not as Pharisees but by other terms, such as scribe or sage, which means rabbi. Despite this identification as scribes, scholars debate whether these were the scribes mentioned in the Gospel accounts. When the Gospel authors mention scribes, we don't actually know if they're referring to groups within the Pharisees' circles or other groups that were separate from them.

- In fact, the beliefs and opinions of the Pharisees eventually became decisive through Rabbinic Judaism after 70 A.D. Their synthesis of free will and determinism and their belief in the sanctity of oral law ultimately prevailed in Judaism.

- The Pharisees were not a monolithic or homogeneous group; in fact, they seem to have been quite diverse. Some of them lived in cities; others came from rural areas. They were made up of the lower ranks of priests, craftspeople, small farmers, and merchants. In a sense, they represented the middle classes.

Immortality and Free Will

- The Pharisees believed in the existence of angels and spirits. Josephus describes the Pharisees as follows: "They also believe that souls have an immortal vigor in them. And that under the Earth, there will be rewards or punishments according as they have lived virtuously or viciously in this life." In Acts of the Apostles 23:8, we read: "For the Sadducees hold that there is no resurrection, and that there are no angels or spirits, while the Pharisees believe in all three."

- The Sadducees believed in complete human free will. The Pharisees, however, emphasized both divine omnipotence and human freedom and responsibility. On the one hand, God is all knowing, but on the other hand, humans still have free will.

- Josephus describes the Pharisees' belief in free will as follows: "And when they determine that all things are done by fate, they do not take away the freedom of men acting as they see fit. Since their notion is that it has pleased God to make a temperament whereby what he wills is done, but so that the will of men can act virtuously or viciously."

- This belief was summed up by Rabbi Akiva, who was also a Pharisee: "All is foreseen, but free will is given."

- Of course, most readers of the Gospel accounts are familiar with the Pharisees and the Sadducees, although most Gospel references are to the Pharisees. One possible reason for this is that Jesus's ministry was based in Galilee, which is where the Pharisees were influential. The Sadducees were based in Jerusalem.

- Another possible reason is that the Pharisees' form of Judaism became dominant after 70 A.D., when the Second Temple was destroyed. The Essenes disappeared from the stage of history at that time, as did the Sadducees. This is the period when it's thought that the Gospels—perhaps except for Mark—were composed.

The Term *Rabbi*
- In a number of passages in the Gospel accounts, Jesus is addressed by the term *rabbi*. The Pharisees sometimes referred to each other as rabbis. According to Mark, "Then Peter said

to Jesus, Rabbi, it is good for us to be here. Let us make three dwellings."

- The term *rabbi* in Hebrew or Aramaic is an unofficial term of respect that was generally given to men who were experts in the Torah, or Jewish law. Literally translated, the term means "my master" or "one who is greater than myself." We should not confuse the term *rabbi* as used in the time of Jesus with modern rabbis.

- Although Pharisees often apparently spoke to each other using the term *rabbi* or were addressed as such because they were considered experts in the law, it doesn't mean that this term was used necessarily only to address someone who was a Pharisee. Anyone who was considered to be an expert in the Torah could have been addressed by the term *rabbi*.

Was Jesus a Pharisee?

- As mentioned earlier, the Pharisaic principle of oral law allowed for interpretation of the written law. But passages in the Gospels suggest that Jesus rejected the principle of oral law.

- For example, Mark 7:1–8 reads: "The Pharisees gathered about him with some scribes who had come from Jerusalem. They had noticed that some of his disciples ate their food without first giving their hands a ceremonial washing to purify them. … And the Pharisees and the scribes asked him, 'Jesus, why do your disciples not observe the rules handed down by our ancestors, but eat food without purifying their hands?'"

- Notice the reference here to the laws handed down by our ancestors—that is, oral law. Jesus's response is very interesting: "But he said to them, it was about you, hypocrites, that Isaiah prophesied. So finally in the words this people honors me with their lips, but their hearts are far from me. In vain do they worship me, teaching human precepts as doctrines."

Lecture 12—Was Jesus a Pharisee? | 79

- Jesus is citing Isaiah 29:13. We see this all throughout the Gospels: Jesus cites passages from the Hebrew Bible to support his position. And Jesus then continues in this passage, saying, "You abandon the commandment of God and hold to human tradition."

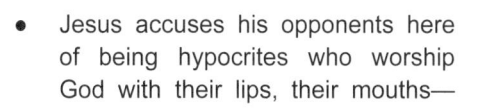

- Jesus accuses his opponents here of being hypocrites who worship God with their lips, their mouths—

> Jesus's accusation that the Pharisees had abandoned the law of God by holding to "human tradition"—oral law rather than written law—strongly suggests that he was not a Pharisee.

in oral tradition—not with their hearts. And he accuses them of improperly following the law by adhering to human traditions. Here, *human traditions* refers to the oral interpretation of the law, not the written law.

- In other words, if we take seriously this passage and others in the Gospel accounts, then we conclude that Jesus was not a Pharisee, and he explicitly rejected the Pharisees' doctrine of oral law.

Suggested Reading

Cohen, *From the Maccabees to the Mishnah*, "Pharisees, Sadducees, and Essenes," pp. 143–164.

Nickelsburg, *Ancient Judaism and Christian Origins*, "Religious Groups," pp. 160–175.

VanderKam, *An Introduction to Early Judaism*, "Groups," pp. 186–192.

Questions to Consider

1. Who were the Sadducees, and what are our sources of information about them?

2. Who were the Pharisees, and how did their beliefs differ from those of the Sadducees?

Lecture

13 Jewish Ritual Purity: The Sons of Light

Jewish ritual purity was fundamental to the lifestyle and beliefs of the Essene sect that lived at Qumran and deposited the Dead Sea Scrolls in the nearby caves. In this lecture, we discuss the initial discovery of the Dead Sea Scrolls and how they came to be known by to the world, examine the site of Qumran itself, explore the practices and beliefs of the Essenes, and analyze the principles and system of Jewish ritual purity.

Discovery of the Dead Sea Scrolls

- The Dead Sea Scrolls are ancient scrolls that were discovered in caves surrounding the site of Qumran, which is located on the northwest shore of the Dead Sea. In 1947, a Bedouin boy wandered into a cave in the vicinity of the site of Qumran and reportedly found a row of tall cylindrical pottery jars, covered with bowl-shaped lids. Inside the jars were ancient scrolls. He alerted the tribe, and the Bedouin then removed these scrolls from the cave.

- The cave that yielded the first scrolls is referred to as Cave 1 at Qumran. Eventually, the Bedouin removed seven complete or nearly complete scrolls from Cave 1. Because the scrolls were written on parchment, which is

> There are several different versions of the story of the discovery of the Dead Sea Scrolls, which were found in large ceramic jars in caves surrounding the site of Qumran.

processed animal hide, they thought at first that they were simply pieces of old leather.

- The Bedouin took the seven scrolls and sold them to a cobbler, Kando, in the area of Bethlehem. Kando did not know that these were ancient scrolls, but he could see that there was writing on at least some of them. Although he could not read the writing, he thought that it resembled the script of his own church, the Syrian Orthodox Church. Kando took four of the scrolls and offered them for sale to the metropolitan of the Syrian Orthodox Church in Jerusalem at that time, Athanasius Yeshue Samuel.

- The other three scrolls Kando offered for sale to Eleazar Lipa Sukenik, a Jewish scholar and archaeologist based at the Hebrew University of Jerusalem. Although we do not know this for sure, Sukenik may have been the first scholar to recognize that the artifacts were, indeed, authentic ancient scrolls dating to about the time of Jesus. Sukenik purchased the three scrolls from Kando.

- In the meantime, Athanasius Yeshue Samuel had purchased his four scrolls as an investment and tried, without success, to sell them for a profit in the markets of the Middle East. Eventually, he put them up for sale in the United States. In 1954, Samuel placed an ad in the *Wall Street Journal*, advertising his four scrolls for sale. It just so happened that Yigael Yadin, the son of Eleazar Sukenik, was in the United States at that time and arranged to purchase the four scrolls.

- Eventually, all seven scrolls from Cave 1 at Qumran came to be in the possession of the State of Israel. Subsequently, Israel erected a special building on the grounds of the Israel Museum in Jerusalem, called the Shrine of the Book, to house and display the scrolls.

Excavation of Qumran

- In the early 1950s, an archaeological expedition was organized to Qumran. The goal of the expedition was to systematically explore all the caves in the area to see if there were any more scrolls left to be found and to excavate the site of Qumran itself. Qumran was a small ruin that was ringed by the caves that eventually yielded all the Dead Sea Scrolls.

- The expedition to Qumran was organized and led by a French biblical scholar and archaeologist named Roland de Vaux. De Vaux was affiliated with the École biblique, the French school of biblical studies and archaeology in East Jerusalem.

- Eventually, scrolls were found in 11 caves surrounding Qumran, which are numbered as caves 1 through 11. Approximately half the scrolls were discovered by Bedouin, and the other half were discovered by archaeologists. Altogether, these 11 caves yielded the remains of approximately 1,000 different scrolls. These scrolls consist mainly of small fragments surviving from what were originally complete documents.

- The other component of de Vaux's expedition was the excavation of the site of Qumran itself. He discovered a small settlement that dated to the 1st century B.C. and 1st century A.D., up until its destruction by the Romans in 68 A.D. The Dead Sea Scrolls represent a collection of literature belonging to members of a Jewish sect who lived at the site of Qumran.

- The site of Qumran itself is characterized by many features that distinguish it from other contemporary settlements. For example, it is clear that the inhabitants lived a communal lifestyle and held communal meals. It is also clear that the inhabitants of Qumran were concerned with maintaining a high degree of Jewish ritual purity. For example, the site has a large number of Jewish ritual baths, called *miqva'ot*.

Jewish Ritual Purity

- Jewish ritual purity is not well understood by most modern Westerners—including most modern Jews. The Torah describes certain categories of things and certain natural processes that cause ritual impurity. However, the causes of ritual impurity, according to biblical law, appear to us today to be quite random.

- No one has ever been able to explain why it is that certain actions and functions cause ritual impurity versus others that do not. The system of ritual purity and impurity is difficult for us to understand today and remains quite controversial among scholars.

- For example, touching a lizard makes one ritually impure, as does touching mildew on the walls of a house and touching a human corpse. Certain natural processes of the human body also cause ritual impurity—for example, nocturnal emissions in men and childbirth and menses in women.

- For most Jews and for most types of ritual impurity, the way to purify oneself is immersion in a pool of what the Bible calls "living water." Jews came to understand the phrase "living water" to refer to undrawn water—a river, stream, lake, or pond—as opposed to water in a pool that had been deliberately dug and filled.
    - To observe these ritual purity laws, living on the shore of the Dead Sea, in an extremely arid climate, would have been a huge challenge for the Jews at Qumran. They devised an elaborate system to bring flood waters to fill up pools at the settlement.

    - The large number of pools and their great size are a clear indication of the Jews' concern with the maintenance of ritual purity and the observance of purity laws.

In the Presence of God

- The kind of ritual purity described here applies primarily to those coming into contact with the presence of God. Basically, Jewish purity laws regulate the admission into God's presence—the divine presence. According to biblical law, when one entered God's presence, one had to be in a state of ritual purity.

- In ancient Judaism, the presence of God dwelt in his house—the Temple of Jerusalem. Therefore, all Jews, including Jesus and Paul, took for granted the fact that when they entered the Jerusalem Temple, they first had to be in a state of ritual purity. But otherwise, most Jews, on an everyday basis, did not have to worry about being in this state. In fact, most Jews were not concerned with ritual purity.

- There was, of course, one category of ancient Jew who had to be concerned with the observance of a high level of ritual purity on a more regular basis: the priests who served in the Temple of Jerusalem. These priests were in God's presence more regularly than other Jews; they were the intermediaries between the Jewish people and the God of Israel.

- The members of the Qumran sect adopted a priestly lifestyle; they followed the laws, including the laws of purity, that applied to priests. The reason for this was that they believed that God's presence dwelled in their midst and angels walked among them.

The System of *Miqva'ot*

- Jewish ritual purity laws applied only to Jews. Gentiles were completely outside the system of laws, because Gentiles were not allowed to enter the presence of the God of Israel in the Temple of Jerusalem.

- Jews dealing with any products going to the Temple of Jerusalem or its priests also had to be in a state of ritual purity. For example, if you grew agricultural produce that was sent to the priests in the Temple of Jerusalem, that produce had to be produced in a state of ritual purity.

- Interestingly, the system of ritual purity has nothing to do with cleanliness and hygiene in the modern sense of the words. In order to be used for ritual purification, water had to fulfill only the requirement of being "living water." But that didn't mean it had to be clean water.

- We actually see evidence of this at Qumran. There, a system of ritual baths were filled by flash-flood waters brought by a nearby riverbed. These pools were filled only once or twice a year, in the winter, on very rare occasions. Over the course of the rest of the year, the pools were used repeatedly by the members of the community for ritual immersion, as well as other purposes, including laundering clothes and drinking. In other words, the process of ritual immersion probably helped spread disease.

Suggested Reading

Magness, *The Archaeology of Qumran and the Dead Sea Scrolls*, chapters 2–3, "The Discovery of the Dead Sea Scrolls and the Exploration of Qumran" and "The Dead Sea Scrolls and the Community at Qumran."

———, *The Archaeology of the Holy Land*, chapter 6, "The Archaeology of Qumran and the Dead Sea Scrolls."

Questions to Consider

1. Who discovered the Dead Sea Scrolls, and where were they found?

2. What are the causes of ritual impurity according to biblical Jewish law, and what are the means of purification?

Lecture

14   The Dead Sea Scrolls: Earliest Hebrew Bible

One of the reasons the Dead Sea Scrolls are so renowned is that they are associated with Jesus in the popular imagination. The Dead Sea Scrolls, however, have nothing directly to do with Jesus himself. The scrolls, sometimes described as the most important archaeological discovery of the 20th century, represent a corpus of literature that belonged to a Jewish sect that lived at Qumran in the 1st century B.C. and 1st century A.D. In this lecture, we will explore why the Dead Sea Scrolls are valuable for understanding Jesus within his broader Jewish context.

Description and Contents of the Scrolls

- Many of the Dead Sea Scrolls were not written or copied at Qumran but were brought to Qumran from elsewhere. Some scrolls antedate the establishment of the settlement at Qumran, but others date to the time when Qumran was occupied by members of this Jewish sect. What we have at Qumran is a mixture of literary works, some of which were brought to the site from elsewhere and some of which may have been written or copied at the site itself.

- Most of the Dead Sea Scrolls were written on parchment, which is processed animal hide. A small number of them were written on papyrus. The majority of the scrolls were written in Hebrew. There is also a large minority of scrolls that were written in Aramaic and a very small number of scrolls written in Greek.

- What is distinctive about the Dead Sea Scrolls is that the entire corpus consists of Jewish religious works—that is, works of the Hebrew Bible and relating to the Hebrew Bible and works relating to the lifestyle and beliefs of the religious sect that lived at Qumran.

- Among the major groups of literature represented in the Dead Sea Scrolls are copies of the Hebrew Bible, or the Old Testament. In fact, all the books of the Hebrew Bible are represented, with the exception of the Book of Esther.
  - These copies of books of the Hebrew Bible—which are fragments, not complete copies—are significant because they represent the earliest copies of the Hebrew Bible that have ever been found. Until the discovery of the Dead Sea Scrolls, the earliest known copies of the Hebrew Bible dated to the 9th and 10th centuries A.D. The copies of the Hebrew Bible from Qumran date mostly to the 2nd and 1st centuries B.C. The Dead Sea Scrolls give us an opportunity to compare the text of the ancient Hebrew Bible with the text that we have today.

  - Today, when you open up a copy of the Hebrew Bible in Hebrew, you will find the same identical text, word for word, letter for letter. This is the standard authoritative text of the Hebrew Bible, called the Masoretic text. But in the time of Jesus, variant versions of the Hebrew Bible circulated among the Jewish population. It wasn't until after the time of Jesus, after the destruction of the Second Temple in 70 A.D., that one standard, authoritative version of the Hebrew Bible came to be used by all Jews.

  - The copies of the Hebrew Bible at Qumran represent not only the proto-Masoretic text—that is, the text that served as the basis for the later Masoretic text—but also variant texts that are not preserved elsewhere.

- The finds at Qumran also include fragments of the Septuagint, the ancient translation of the Hebrew Bible into Greek. By the Hellenistic period, after the conquest of Alexander the Great, many Diaspora Jews no longer were able to read and understand Hebrew; instead, they read and spoke Greek. It was against this background that the Hebrew Bible was translated into Greek.

- Also at Qumran is a category of literature called Targum, an ancient translation of the Hebrew Bible into Aramaic. Aramaic is related to Hebrew, but by the time of Jesus, the common, everyday language of the Jewish population was Aramaic, not Hebrew.

Pesharim

- Another category of work represented among the Dead Sea Scrolls that is related to the Hebrew Bible is a *pesher*, or in the plural, *pesharim*. A *pesher* is a commentary on or interpretation of a book of the Hebrew Bible. Usually, it is a commentary on a prophetic book.

- What is distinctive about the genre of *pesher* found at Qumran is that the author interpreted biblical passages in light of events that were happening in his own time.

- The second distinctive feature of the *pesher* works is that the author believed that the true meaning of these biblical passages had been revealed through an inspired teacher, a leader of the Qumran sect who is referred to as the Teacher of Righteousness.

Apocrypha and Pseudepigrapha

- Yet another category of Jewish religious literature represented among the Dead Sea Scrolls is Apocrypha. The word means "hidden books" and refers to books that were included in the Catholic canon of sacred scripture but not in the Jewish or Protestant canon. Represented among the Dead Sea Scrolls is the Book of Tobit and Ecclesiasticus, or the Wisdom of Ben Sira.

- A category of literature related to biblical works is Pseudepigrapha, meaning "false writings." This term refers to the common practice of an author attributing his work to someone else to give it greater authority.

- Pseudepigrapha are Jewish religious works of this period that were not included in the Jewish, Protestant, or Catholic canon

In the wake of the Heliodorus affair, various branches of the Zadokite family dispersed in different directions; the Oniads went to Egypt, the Sadducees stayed in Jerusalem, and the remaining branch became instrumental in founding the sect at Qumran.

of sacred literature. But they were sometimes preserved in the canons of other churches, such as the Ethiopian church. Examples of Pseudepigrapha from Qumran are the Book of Enoch and the Book of Jubilees.

Sectarian Works

- The final category of literature found among the Dead Sea Scrolls are sectarian works—writings that describe the beliefs and practices of the sect that lived at Qumran and deposited the scrolls in the nearby caves. These scrolls provide information about the history of the sect, their lifestyle, and their beliefs and practices.

- The sectarian scrolls suggest that the sect formed initially somewhere in the first half of the 2nd century B.C., against the background of the turbulent events leading up to the Maccabean Revolt. Specifically, the scrolls suggest that this sect was initially founded by dispossessed Zadokite priests.

- The Zadokite priests were a group of high priests who controlled the sacrificial cult in the Temple of Jerusalem until the time of the Heliodorus affair. They traced their ancestry back to a man named Zadok—or, in Hebrew, Zadoc.

- Through the complicated series of events connected with the Heliodorus affair, the Zadokites lost control of the high priesthood and became dispossessed. In other words, at Qumran, we seem to have members of a sect that was founded by dispossessed Zadokite priests.

The Teacher of Righteousness

- The Dead Sea Scrolls tell us that the sect at Qumran was initially led by a founder called the Teacher of Righteousness. One of the interesting characteristics of the sectarian scrolls is that they refer to historical figures not by their actual names but, instead, by nicknames. These nicknames are usually puns. Therefore,

"Teacher of Righteousness" is a nickname for the founder of the Qumran sect.

- In Hebrew, "Teacher of Righteousness" is *moreh ha-tzedek*. Notice that "righteousness" in Hebrew is *tzedek*. It is a pun on Zadok or Zadokite. In other words, the nickname "Teacher of Righteousness" suggests that this figure was, in fact, one of the dispossessed Zadokite high priests. Although there has been a great deal of scholarly speculation about this issue, the nickname is a strong indicator about his identity.

- Similarly, the main opponent of the Teacher of Righteousness mentioned in the Dead Sea Scrolls is a figure called the Wicked Priest. "Wicked Priest" is also a pun in Hebrew. The words *ha-kohen ha-rasha* are a pun on *ha-kohen ha-rashi* (or *roshe*). In other words, the "Wicked Priest" is a pun in Hebrew on the high priest. The opponent of the Teacher of Righteousness was the current high priest officiating in the Temple of Jerusalem.

An Apocalyptic Sect

- The Dead Sea Scrolls provide a great deal of information about the lifestyle and beliefs of the Qumran sect. Apparently, some members practiced desert separatism—that is, they went apart to live in the desert. While members of the sect were married and had families, some of them may have practiced either occasional or permanent celibacy.

- To apply for full membership in the Qumran sect, one had to be an unblemished adult Jewish male—that is, without physical or mental disabilities or handicaps. To become a full member of the sect, one had to undergo a process of initiation that lasted between two to three years. During the course of that initiation, applicants were admitted in stages—with each stage of membership representing the attainment of a higher level of Jewish ritual purity.

- Full members of the sect lived according to the laws that governed the lifestyle of a priest serving in the Temple of Jerusalem, because the members believed that God was literally dwelling in their midst. This was an apocalyptic sect that believed that the end of days was already underway. And they believed that they were the only ones who would be saved. In this regard, the Qumran sect is similar to Jesus and his movement, who also believed that the end of days was at hand.

- There are interesting similarities and differences between the conception of the end of days among members of the Qumran sect and among Jesus and his movement. We will explore those further in our next lecture.

Suggested Reading
VanderKam, *The Dead Sea Scrolls Today*, chapters 2 and 4, "Survey of the Manuscripts" and "The Scrolls and the Old Testament."

Questions to Consider
1. What are the Dead Sea Scrolls?

2. What do the Dead Sea Scrolls tell us about the Qumran sect?

Lecture

15   Was Jesus an Essene?

In this lecture, we discuss the apocalyptic outlook of the Jewish religious sect that lived at Qumran and deposited the Dead Sea Scrolls in the nearby caves. We will also examine the beliefs and practices of the Essenes and the status of women as members of the sect. In conclusion, we will consider whether Jesus and John the Baptist were Essenes.

The Sons of Light
- The sect at Qumran believed that at the end of days, there would be a 40-year war between the forces of good and evil. This sect called themselves the forces of good—the Sons of Light. Everyone else, including all other Jews, were the Sons of Darkness. One of the peculiarities of this sect is that its members believed in predeterminism—that is, everything is preordained by God. In fact, this sect believed that there was no such thing at all as free will.

- The outcome of the 40-year war between the Sons of Light and the Sons of Darkness was preordained by God: a victory for the Sons of Light. This apocalyptic scenario also involved the arrival of a messianic figure. Specifically, the Dead Sea Scrolls refer to two and perhaps three anticipated messianic figures:
  o A royal messiah descended from David

  o A priestly messiah descended from Aaron

  o A prophetic messiah.

- These beliefs differ from those of Jesus and his followers, who anticipated a single messianic figure. What's more, Jesus's followers essentially came to believe that Jesus combined, in himself, all three aspects of the anticipated messiah—royal, priestly, and prophetic.

- For the Qumran sect, the current apocalyptic era would usher in the rebuilding of an ideal Temple of Jerusalem, which is described in the Temple Scroll.

The Essenes
- Scholars glean much of our information about the Essenes from Flavius Josephus, the Jewish author and historian who lived in the 1st century A.D.; Philo Judaeus, the Jewish philosopher who lived in Alexandria, Egypt, in the late 1st century B.C. and early 1st century A.D.; and Pliny the Elder, the Roman naturalist and historian who lived in the 1st century A.D.

- These authors describe a Jewish sect called the Essenes, and in fact, these Essenes have beliefs and practices that are remarkably similar to what we read about in the Dead Sea Scrolls. Pliny the Elder includes a point of geographical information that is not found in the other ancient authors. Pliny specifically describes the Essenes as living in the area where Qumran is located; he observes, "To the west of the Dead Sea, the Essenes have put the necessary distance between themselves and the insalubrious shore."

- Because of the similarities between these authors' descriptions of the Essenes and what we read in the Dead Sea Scrolls, many scholars identify the sect that lived at Qumran as Essenes. However, the word *Essene* never occurs in the Dead Sea Scrolls. There are at least two possible reasons for this.
    - One is language: Our sources have come down to us in Greek and Latin, whereas the overwhelming majority of the Dead Sea Scrolls are in Hebrew and Aramaic.

    - It is also possible that *Essene* does not occur in the Dead Sea Scrolls because it is not a term the members of the sect used to describe themselves but was used by outsiders. In particular, the Qumran sect called themselves the Sons of Light, the Sons of Zadok, or *yahad*, which means "the unity" or "the community."

The Philosophical Lifestyle

- In studying the descriptions of the Essenes in Philo, Josephus, and Pliny, we note that there is a lack of women in the sect. It is described as a sect of celibate adult men. According to Pliny, the Essenes "are a people unique of its kind and admirable beyond all others in the whole world, without women and renouncing love entirely, without money and having for company only the palm trees."

- However, if we examine the sectarian Dead Sea Scrolls, we see legislation regulating marriage, divorce, childbirth, and the rearing of children. For this reason, some scholars argue that the sect that lived at Qumran could not be the Essenes, because clearly the Dead Sea Scrolls inform us that women were a part of this sect.

- The reason for this discrepancy may be that the Dead Sea Scrolls represent literature that the sect at Qumran used for its own internal purposes, whereas the outside authors were creating a very different category of literature. Josephus and Philo were both Jewish men who lived and wrote in a Diaspora environment, as part of a small Jewish minority in an overwhelmingly Greco-Roman milieu. Although these writers were influenced by the Greco-Roman way of thought, they were also concerned with highlighting the value and importance of Judaism.

- One of the characteristic features of Greco-Roman philosophy is the ideal philosophical lifestyle—that one should live a life of simplicity. Josephus and Philo may have been trying to present the Essenes as a Jewish group that lived this lifestyle. They took a relatively small and obscure sect—the Essenes—and elevated them as a sort of philosophical ideal.

Celibacy and the Status of Women

- Celibacy was not mandated in Jewish law. To the contrary, in Genesis, God says, "Be fruitful and multiply." What's more, members of the Qumran sect lived their everyday lives as if they were priests serving in the Temple of Jerusalem. And Jewish priests were not celibate; they were married and had families.

- However, priests who served in the Temple of Jerusalem served in rotations; that is, for a couple of weeks at a time, they would leave their families and go to serve in the Temple. During that time, they had no contact with their families, because of purity concerns. Perhaps the sect at Qumran left their families behind at certain times and practiced occasional celibacy, like the priests in the Temple of Jerusalem.

- It is quite probable that women could not join the Qumran sect. The Dead Sea Scrolls contain no regulations describing admission procedures for women. Similarly, our outside sources contain no descriptions of how a woman could join the sect. It is likely that women were only able to join the sect by being born into it or marrying someone who was a member of the sect. What's more, it is unlikely that women could attain the same high status as men in the sect, just as women could not serve as priests in the Temple of Jerusalem.

Was Jesus an Essene?

- There are some strong similarities between the Qumran sect—the Essenes—and the movement surrounding Jesus. These similarities include the practices of pooling possessions and holding communal meals. Both movements were apocalyptic and anticipated the imminent arrival of the end of days.

- At the same time, there are also important differences between the Qumran sect and Jesus's movement. The Qumran sect believed that everything is predetermined by God and there is no free will. Jesus certainly did not preach that there is no human free will.

- The Qumran sect anticipated the arrival of two or, perhaps, three messianic figures, whereas Jesus's followers believed that Jesus embodied all three of the messianic aspects: priestly, royal, and prophetic.

- Another key difference is that the Qumran sect adopted a priestly lifestyle. Every full member lived his everyday life as if he were a priest officiating in the Jerusalem Temple, which meant that full members observed the highest level of Jewish ritual purity. But according to the Gospel accounts, Jesus regularly came in contact with members of the Jewish population who were impure. In fact, Jesus's approach to the observance of Jewish purity laws was the polar opposite from the approach of the Qumran sect.

- Another broad difference between the Qumran sect and Jesus's movement is their inclusive versus exclusive approaches. The Qumran sect was an exclusive sect; full membership was not open to the majority of the population. Jesus's approach, however, was inclusive. He welcomed everyone into his movement. These differences strongly suggest that Jesus could not have been an Essene.

John the Baptist

- Although Jesus could not have been an Essene, there is another figure in early Christian tradition who might have been a member of this sect or at least may have had contacts with the Essenes: John the Baptist.

- John the Baptist was from a priestly family that was active in the area close to Qumran—near the Jordan River—at the same time that Qumran was settled by the Jewish religious sect. He lived a simple and ascetic lifestyle. What's more, he is best known for his practice of baptism—that is, immersion in water, which recalls the ritual purification procedures that are characteristic of Judaism in that time and the Essenes in particular.

- However, there are still some significant differences between John the Baptist in the Gospel accounts and the beliefs and

> The practice of baptism, associated with John the Baptist, recalls the ritual purification process characteristic of Judaism, particular the Essene sect, at the time of Jesus.

practices of the Essenes. For one, John's clothing and diet are quite different from what the Essenes wore and ate. According to Matthew 3:4, "Now John wore clothing of camel's hair, with a leather belt around his waist. And his food was locusts and wild honey." By contrast, members of the Essenes wore linen clothing, emulating the clothing of the priests in the Temple of Jerusalem. And they had their own particular pure food and pure drink, not a diet of locusts and honey.

- Although the beliefs and practices of the Essene sect might have had some influence on John, his theology is also quite different. In Judaism, it was necessary to continually repeat the process of ritual purification. The process of becoming ritually impure is unavoidable if you are a human being; at various points in your life, you need to purify yourself again.

- What's more, ritual purification in Judaism is a mechanical process—that is, becoming impure is not associated with being sinful or evil. However, according to the practices of John the Baptist and in later Christianity, baptism becomes a one-time process for cleansing sin.

Suggested Reading
VanderKam, *The Dead Sea Scrolls Today*, chapter 6, "The Scrolls and the New Testament."

Questions to Consider
1. Was Jesus or John the Baptist an Essene?

2. What are the similarities and differences between the Qumran sect and Jesus's movement?

Lecture

16   The Hebrew Scriptures and the Septuagint

Around 200 B.C., during the early Hellenistic period, the Torah—the book of law in the Hebrew Bible—was translated into Greek. This translation was called the Septuagint. At that time, a large Jewish Diaspora community flourished in Egypt, concentrated in Alexandria. In this lecture, we discuss the works of Philo of Alexandria, or Philo Judaeus, a highly educated Jewish philosopher from Alexandria—a Diaspora Jew. We will also examine the differences between the Septuagint and the original Hebrew Bible. Because of these differences, Jews eventually rejected the authority of the Septuagint, while the Christians embraced it.

The "Letter of Aristeas"
- Under the Ptolemies, many Jewish immigrants settled in Alexandria, which was the capital of Egypt and the cultural center of the Hellenistic world. Alexandria was the setting for the "Letter of Aristeas," a literary work composed toward the end of the 2nd century B.C.

- The "Letter of Aristeas" describes the translation of the Torah into Greek. The Greek translation is called the Septuagint (from the Latin *septuaginta*, or "70"). In the "Letter of Aristeas," Aristeas presents himself as a man in the court of Ptolemy II Philadelphus, who was sent to the high priest in Jerusalem in an effort to have the Torah translated from Hebrew to Greek.

- The story begins when Ptolemy II appointed Demetrius of Phaleron to be the librarian at his new royal library in Alexandria. Demetrius aimed at collecting, if possible, all the books in the world. According to the "Letter of Aristeas," Demetrius told the king that the law books of the Jews were worth translation and inclusion in the royal library and requested that they be brought to Alexandria.

- The problem, of course, is that the Torah was in Hebrew, but the language of Alexandria was Greek. Therefore, the king ordered that a letter be sent to the high priest in Jerusalem so that work on the translation could begin.

- According to the "Letter of Aristeas," six learned men from each of the 12 tribes (totaling 72 men, hence, the "70") were brought to Alexandria to carry out the translation. While the story in the "Letter of Aristeas" appears to be fictional, it is a fact that the Torah was translated into Greek sometime in the early Hellenistic period, around 200 B.C.

- In addition to the "Letter of Aristeas," scholars have other sources of information about the Jewish Diaspora community. For example, in later rabbinic literature, there is a description of the great synagogue of Alexandria.
    - Although we do not have any archaeological remains of this synagogue, a description is given in the Jerusalem Talmud. The passage notes that the great synagogue in Alexandria was a large basilica with gold furniture in it, suggesting a large and prosperous Jewish community.
    - The Talmud passage also says that the people were seated according to their crafts or guilds. This suggests an organization based on voluntary association, which was characteristic of the Greek and Roman worlds.

Philo of Alexandria

- Within the Alexandria Diaspora community, there was perhaps no figure more significant than Philo of Alexandria, or Philo Judaeus, who lived from approximately 20 B.C. to 50 A.D. He is one of our key sources of information about the Essenes.

- Philo was a wealthy, highly educated Jewish philosopher, who was born and raised and spent his entire life in Alexandria. He is known to us because his works are well-preserved. One of the characteristic features of Philo's works is that he sought to ascertain the literal and allegorical meaning of the Hebrew Bible, which he believed to be the source of all truth.

- Specifically, Philo applied allegory when the literal meaning of biblical passages did not make sense or used it to resolve contradictions and questions. He wrote: "The exposition of sacred scripture proceeds by unfolding the meaning hidden in allegories, for the entire law is regarded by these persons as resembling an animal. And for its body it has the literal precepts, but for its soul the unseen reason hidden away in the words."

- Philo's outlook and philosophy were definitely steeped in Greek philosophy—specifically Platonic philosophy. We see that very clearly expressed in the way that he attempts to understand biblical text. Another characteristic of Philo's works is that he often alludes to the *logos*, which again, refers to Greek philosophy and philosophical thought. In Philo, the *logos* is an intermediary divine being that bridges the gap between God and the material world.

Philo's allegorical method of interpreting the Bible was clearly influenced by Plato and became useful to later Christians.

- Philo's writings were preserved by the Christians, who admired his allegorical interpretations of the Bible and use of the concept of the *logos*.

- In addition to being a valuable source of information on the Essenes, Philo describes another Jewish sect with an ascetic lifestyle: the Therapeutae. Their existence is controversial, however, because we have no archaeological remains associated with them, nor do any other ancient authors describe them. Philo is our only source.

Pogrom against the Jews

- During Philo's lifetime, a number of significant events occurred in Alexandria. Perhaps the most disturbing was in 38 A.D., when a pogrom targeted the Jews. Non-Jewish inhabitants rioted, burning and sacking Jewish homes, shops, and synagogues.

- After the pogrom, the Roman governor dissolved the *politeuma* of the Jews, which had been in place since Ptolemaic times. The *politeuma* was a constitution that granted the Jews political and religious rights and a certain amount of autonomy in Alexandria.

- In 38 or 39 A.D., the Jewish population of Alexandria sent a delegation to the Roman emperor in order to appeal to him. The emperor at that time was Gaius Caligula, and the Jewish delegation was headed by Philo. But in addition to the Jewish delegation, there was also a delegation of Alexandrian non-Jews that was led by a man named Apion, a well-known hater of the Jews.

- Flavius Josephus wrote a book titled *Against Apion*, which contains this relevant passage:

    On the Jewish residents of Alexandria, Apion emphasized their foreign origin and their separate residence and questioned their right to be called Alexandrians. ... Their refusal to honor Alexandrian gods and their responsibility for recent disturbances made absurd the claim of some to be Alexandrian citizens, and their failure to pay typical honors to the emperor made them all politically suspect to the Empire.

The Septuagint
- Although Philo's writings seem quite Hellenized and influenced by a Greek philosophical worldview, he strove to emphasize the importance of the Torah. When the Torah was translated into Greek sometime in the early Hellenistic period, Jews of the Hellenistic world (many of whom no longer spoke or read Hebrew) were able to gain access to their scriptures. What's more, the translation made the Torah accessible to a wider audience.

- Of particular significance is the fact that the Greek translation of the Hebrew Bible—called the Septuagint version—often varies with the original Hebrew text. Because of the differences between the two texts, after the destruction of the Second Temple, the Jews began to deny the authority of the Septuagint. Eventually, Jews began to produce rival translations, such as that of Aquila, for the needs of Diaspora Jews.

- Another reason the Jews rejected the authority of the Septuagint translation is that it remained the Greek Bible for the Christian church. As Christianity began to grow and spread, its followers used the Septuagint translation. Much later, at the time of the Reformation, Protestants appealed to the authority of the Hebrew original, but the Septuagint has remained the authoritative text for the Catholic Church.

A Question of Translation
- We conclude with a discussion of the problems of translation, which may shed some light on why the Jews eventually came to reject the authority of the Septuagint. Consider this significant passage from Isaiah 7:14: "Therefore the Lord himself will give

you a sign; behold, a young woman is with child, and is about to bear a son, and she will call him Immanuel."

- In Hebrew, *almah* means "young woman." But the Septuagint version translates *almah* as *parthenos*. *Parthenos*, in Greek, also means "young woman," but it also can mean "virgin." Notice, in Matthew 1:23, this citation of that same passage in Isaiah: "The maiden [*parthenos*] will be pregnant and will have a son, and they will name him Immanuel."

- *Parthenos* could have simply meant "young woman," but it could also be understood as "virgin," which is how Christians came to understand that term. And, of course, this passage holds great significance for Christians, who celebrate the virgin birth of Jesus.

Suggested Reading

Goldenberg, *The Origins of Judaism*, chapter 6, "Diaspora and Homeland."

Schiffman, *Texts and Traditions*, "The Literature of the Hellenistic Diaspora," pp. 203–230.

Questions to Consider

1. Why were Philo's writings preserved by Christians?

2. What is the importance of the Greek translation of the Pentateuch?

Lecture

17 The Reign of Herod the Great

By the middle of the 2nd century B.C., the Romans had expanded their control into the eastern Mediterranean. In 63 B.C., the Romans took over the area around Israel and annexed the Hasmonean kingdom to Rome. In 40 B.C., the Parthians—successors to the ancient Persians—reestablished the Hasmonean kingdom, installing Mattathias Antigonus as the king of Judea. At the same time, Judea was under the administration of Hyrcanus II, the high priest, who was assisted by Herod. These men were governing Judea on behalf of the Romans. In this lecture, we review the reign of Herod the Great and conclude by discussing the Massacre of the Innocents, an atrocity for which Herod is remembered above all others.

The Decapolis
- The Hasmonean dynasty ruled the kingdom in Israel in the second half of the 2nd century B.C. and the first half of the 1st century B.C. Salome Alexandra, the widow of Alexander Jannaeus, had succeeded him to the throne after he died in 76 B.C. Salome Alexandra ruled until 67 B.C. During her reign, her older son, Hyrcanus II, served as high priest in the Temple of Jerusalem. But after she died, a civil war erupted over the succession to the throne between her sons Hyrcanus II and Aristobulus II.

- This civil war provided the Romans with an ideal opportunity to step in and take over the country, which they did in 63 B.C., annexing the Hasmonean kingdom to Rome. The Romans paid special attention to the most Hellenized cities, which they believed would be most loyal to Rome. To strengthen them, they formed them into a league called the Decapolis, which in Greek means "league of 10 cities."

- The Decapolis cities were under the direct administration of the newly established Roman province of Syria. In 40 B.C., when the

Parthians overran the area, they reestablished the Hasmonean kingdom, with Mattathias Antigonus as its king. At this time, Judea was administered by Hyrcanus II, the high priest, who was assisted by Herod and his older brother Phasael. Herod and Phasael were Idumean Jews through forced conversion on their grandfather's side of the family.

Herod's Early Reign in Judea

- In 40 B.C., Herod fled the country by way of Alexandria and made his way to Rome, where, with the support of Mark Antony, the Roman Senate approved Herod as king of Judea. This time was a period in Roman history called the Late Republic, when the Roman Republic was dissolving, and power was divided up among different generals—among them, Mark Antony.

- Herod returned from Rome with the authority to rule Judea as king on behalf of the Romans. He spent the next three years fighting Mattathias Antigonus and his forces until, finally, in 37 B.C., Jerusalem fell.

- The early years of Herod's reign were characterized by his efforts to reestablish rule. Even though Mattathias Antigonus had been eliminated, there would be further attempts by the Hasmoneans to regain authority.

- One of the problems that Herod had with Hasmoneans at this point is that they were now part of his own household. While Herod had numerous wives, his most famous was a Hasmonean princess named Mariamne. Mariamne's mother, Alexandra, sought to reestablish Hasmonean rule through her daughter.

- When it came time to appoint the high priest in the Temple of Jerusalem, instead of choosing a member of the Hasmonean household, because he feared opposition, Herod appointed an undistinguished Babylonian priest named Hananel. This infuriated his mother-in-law, Alexandra, by passing over her son, Aristobulus III.

Murder of Aristobulus III

- Alexandra then contacted Cleopatra in Egypt to enlist her help in having Mark Antony force Herod to appoint her son to the post. Cleopatra was a threat to Herod from the very beginning of his reign because she coveted Herod's kingdom. Of course, by this point, Cleopatra was involved with Mark Antony.

- Alexandra's strategy worked—at first. Antony showed an interest in Aristobulus III, and Herod capitulated and replaced Hananel with Aristobulus III, who was only 17 years old. Aristobulus III took office, presiding as high priest over the holiday of Sukkot, the Feast of Tabernacles. According to Josephus, Aristobulus was well-loved by the people: "And so there arose among the people an impulsive feeling of affection for him .... They called out to him good wishes mingled with prayers."

- Herod's worst fears were realized. Herod himself was insecure about his position as king of Judea because he was not descended from the Hasmoneans. He was afraid of the support that the Hasmoneans had among the Jewish population. When Aristobulus inspired a wave of affection and support from the people, Herod reacted.

- Josephus tells the rest of the story: "For although he had given him the high priesthood at the age of 17, he killed him quickly after he had conferred that dignity upon him." What's more, four years later, in 31 B.C., Herod also had Hyrcanus II put to death. This left Mariamne the pivotal Hasmonean in Herod's personal life.

Cleopatra and Mark Antony

- Cleopatra—specifically, Cleopatra VII—was a descendant of the Ptolemies, whose kingdom had also been absorbed by Rome. In 37 or 36 B.C., Cleopatra married Mark Antony. At this point, Mark Antony was administering the eastern half of the Mediterranean on behalf of Rome. He set up his base of operations in Alexandria in Egypt, and that's where he met and fell in love with Cleopatra.

- As a descendant of the Ptolemies, Cleopatra believed that she had the right to rule over the kingdom that Herod had been given. And she nibbled away, as best as she could, at Herod's kingdom, getting Mark Antony to give her bits and pieces of it over the course of the years.

- Mark Anthony's co-ruler was a man named Octavian, later known as Augustus. Anthony became involved with Cleopatra in Egypt while he was married to Octavian's sister, Octavia. Eventually, he divorced Octavia and married Cleopatra. All these events contributed to tensions between Antony and Octavian, leading to the Battle of Actium in 31 B.C.

Battle of Actium

- The Battle of Actium was a naval battle fought off the coast of Greece between the forces of Mark Antony and Cleopatra, on the one hand, and the forces of Octavian, on the other. Octavian decisively defeated Antony and Cleopatra. After the battle, Antony and Cleopatra went back to Egypt, where they both committed suicide, paving the way for Octavian to become sole ruler of all the lands of Rome.

- After the Battle of Actium, Herod met with Octavian on the island of Rhodes and persuaded the Roman ruler to allow him to remain king of Judea. Herod was so convincing that not only did Octavian reconfirm him as king, but Herod returned to Judea with even greater honor and freedom of action. Octavian granted him additional territories to rule over, expanding the size of Herod's kingdom.

- Just a few years later, in 27 B.C., the Roman Senate bestowed upon Octavian the title of Augustus, formally bringing to an end the period of Roman history that we call the republic and beginning the period of the empire.

Among Herod the Great's construction projects was the rebuilding of a small town on the coast of Palestine called Straton's Tower, which he named in honor of Augustus: Caesarea Maritima.

Herod's Return to Judea

- When Herod traveled to Rhodes to meet with Octavian after the Battle of Actium, he placed Mariamne, Alexandra, and his children under armed guard. When he returned in 29 B.C., he suspected that Mariamne had had an affair with her guard.

- Josephus reports to us Herod's actions: "Then out of his ungovernable jealousy and rage, he commanded both of them to be killed immediately. But as soon as his passion was over, he repented of what he had done. And as soon as his anger was worn off, his affections were kindled again. Indeed, the flames of his desires for her were so ardent that he could not think she was dead, but he would appear under his disorders to speak to her as if she were alive."

- At the same time that Herod was murdering most of his family, he also sponsored numerous building projects. In fact, Herod is known as the single greatest builder in the history of the land of

Israel. He rebuilt the Second Temple in Jerusalem, which was completed in 62–64 A.D., long after Herod's death.

Massacre of the Innocents

- Before Mariamne was put to death by Herod, she bore him five children. Two of those children were sons, Alexander and Aristobulus. In 17 B.C., they returned to Jerusalem from their schooling in Rome, and Herod arranged marriages for them. Because they were Hasmonean princes, they were popular among the local Jewish population. Some of Herod's non-Hasmonean relatives viewed them as a threat and led a campaign of slander against them.

- Herod, being paranoid, believed the rumors, and in 12 B.C., he denounced Alexander and Aristobulus, accused them of treason, and imprisoned them. A few years later, in 7 B.C., he had them murdered.

- Herod's murder of his own sons brings to mind an infamous episode in the Gospels, the Massacre of the Innocents. As reported in Matthew 2:

    > After Jesus' birth in Bethlehem of Judea, during the reign of King Herod, astrologers from the East arrived one day in Jerusalem inquiring, "Where is the newborn King of the Jews? We observed his star at its rising and have come to pay him homage." At this, King Herod became greatly disturbed, and with him all Jerusalem. Once Herod realized that he had been deceived by the astrologers, he became furious. He ordered the massacre of all the boys two years and under in Bethlehem and its environs, making his calculations on the basis of the date he had learned from the astrologers.

- The Massacre of the Innocents is probably the episode for which Herod is best known, but many scholars believe that it is not historical. If that is the case, then perhaps what underlies this episode is Herod's reputation for killing his own sons.

Suggested Reading

Magness, *The Archaeology of the Holy Land*, chapters 7–8.

Schiffman, *Texts and Traditions*, "Herodian Rule," pp. 385–395.

Questions to Consider

1. What internal and external threats did Herod face during the early years of his reign?

2. What might be the basis for the story of the Massacre of the Innocents as related by Matthew?

Lecture

18 Pontius Pilate: A Roman Prefect

In 4 B.C., King Herod the Great died of an agonizing illness. In this lecture, we discuss the division of Herod's kingdom after his death, followed by the introduction of direct Roman administration through prefects, the most famous of whom was Pontius Pilate. Herod's death and the division of his kingdom set us up for a series of events that in the coming decades would lead to the outbreak of the First Jewish Revolt against the Romans, which culminated in the destruction of the Second Temple in Jerusalem in 70 A.D.

Division of Herod's Kingdom

- When Herod the Great died, his kingdom was divided among three of his sons—all of whom were named Herod.
  - Herod Archelaus ruled from 4 B.C. until 6 A.D. over Judea, Samaria, and Idumea—the core part of the Jewish and Yahwist area.

  - Herod Antipas ruled until 39 A.D. over the area of Galilee and Perea.

  - Until his death in 33 or 34 A.D., Herod Philip ruled over the far northern territories of Herod's kingdom—that is, the area of the Golan and parts of modern-day Syria. Herod Philip's part of the kingdom consisted of territories that were largely Gentile.

- Of the three sons, Herod Archelaus had by far the shortest reign. Because he was an incompetent ruler, in 6 A.D., the Romans removed him and banished him to Gaul—modern-day France. At that point, the Romans placed the administration of Herod Archelaus's territories under the administration of a low-ranking Roman governor who reported directly to the legate in the Syria district.

- This governor now moved the base of his administration from Jerusalem to Caesarea Maritima, a city on the coast that became the military headquarters and administrative capital. Caesarea was a good choice because it was a Romanized city and because, on the coast, it had easy communications with Rome by way of the Mediterranean Sea.

- Thus, there was no major concentration of Roman troops in the area around Israel. Because only a legate could command a legion, the troops would have been stationed in Antioch to the north, where the Roman legate was based. This is a key fact, because when trouble started to break out in the region, there is no large concentration of Roman troops nearby to address it.

Murder of John the Baptist

- Of the three sons of Herod, Herod Antipas had the longest reign. He divorced his wife to marry Herodias, the wife of his half-brother Philip. In doing so, however, Herod Antipas transgressed biblical law, which forbids marriage to a brother's wife.

- Herod Antipas is notorious for having executed John the Baptist. Interestingly, the Gospel writers portray the execution of John the Baptist by Herod Antipas in connection with his marriage to Herodias. Here is the relevant passage from Matthew 14:3–12: "For Herod had seized John and bound him and put him in prison on account of Herodias, his brother Philip's wife. For John said to him, it is not right for you to be living with her."

- This event is also reported in Mark and Luke. In other words, according to the Gospel authors, John the Baptist was put to death by Herod Antipas for condemning his biblically illegal marriage to his brother's wife.

- Flavius Josephus also reports the execution of John the Baptist by Herod Antipas, but he provides a different reason: "Herod decided, therefore, that it would be much better to strike first and be rid of him before his work led to an uprising than to wait for an upheaval, get involved in a difficult situation, and see his mistake." According to Josephus, Herod Antipas was motivated by fear that John the Baptist was stirring up trouble.

Pontius Pilate

- Pontius Pilate was fifth in a series of low-ranking Roman governors who were put in charge of administering Judea after Herod Archelaus was removed in 6 A.D. Pilate administered the area from 26 to 36 A.D. It was during his administration that tensions between the Jews and the Romans reached the breaking point.

- Philo of Alexandria describes Pilate as "naturally inflexible, a blend of self-will and relentlessness" and speaks of his conduct as full of "briberies, insults, robberies, outrages, and wanton injuries, executions without trial constantly repeated, ceaseless and supremely grievous cruelty."

- An example of Pilate's incompetence can be seen in one aspect of his treatment of the Jews: Pilate's predecessors had stationed troops in Jerusalem whose military standards were not decorated with medallion busts of the emperor, because they knew that this would offend the Jews. Pilate, however, sent troops into Jerusalem by night carrying effigies of the emperor. When confronted by crowds of protesters, he finally withdrew them.

- Thus, Jesus's death at the hands of Pontius Pilate should be seen as the suppression of what Pilate felt was a potentially threatening situation.

- Repeatedly, we find these low-ranking Roman governors overreacting to situations that they felt were potentially threatening. An episode in Luke relates to the way that the Romans were now administering the country. Remember, at this point, Antipas is administering the area of Galilee and Perea in the north. In other words, during Jesus's ministry, the area of

Galilee was under the administration of Herod Antipas, the son of Herod the Great.
- Here is the description in Luke 23:4–12: "And Pilate said to the high priests and the crowd, I cannot find anything criminal about this man. But they persisted and said, he is stirring up people all over Judea by his teaching. He began in Galilee and he has come here." Jesus began his ministry in Galilee, the area administered by Herod Antipas, but now he was in Judea in Jerusalem, which was under the administration of Pontius Pilate.

- The passage from Luke continues: "When Pilate heard this, he asked if the man was a Galilean. And learning that he belonged to Herod's jurisdiction, he turned him over to Herod, for Herod was in Jerusalem at that time. And Herod and his guards made light of him and ridiculed him. And they put a gorgeous robe on him and sent him back to Pilate. And Herod and Pilate became friends that day, for they had been at enmity before."

- Eventually, Pilate was dismissed after a clash with a large group of armed Samaritans, who had traveled to Mount Gerizim, expecting to find the sacred tabernacle vessels hidden there by Moses. Pilate, probably fearing some underlying military purpose, had his troops block the procession of pilgrims. A battle ensued, with casualties, and Pilate executed the ringleader and the most influential Samaritans. The Samaritans then appealed to the local legate based in Antioch, who ordered Pilate to Rome for trial and replaced him with another prefect.

Herod Agrippa I and Gaius Caligula
- Herod Agrippa I was the grandson of King Herod the Great and his Hasmonean wife Mariamne. Like many other princes throughout the Roman provinces, Herod Agrippa I was raised and educated in Rome. As a young boy growing up in Rome, he was a childhood friend of Gaius Caligula, who became emperor

in 37 A.D. Herod Agrippa I's childhood friendship with Gaius Caligula eventually stood him in good stead.

- Although Caligula is infamous in Roman history for having been extremely cruel, in the beginning, he was actually an effective ruler and quite popular. According to Flavius Josephus, however, "As time went on, he ceased to think of himself as a man, and as he imagined himself a god because of the greatness of his empire, he was moved to disregard the divine power in all his official acts."

- When Gaius Caligula proclaimed himself a god, the Jews in Egypt became objects of abuse from their Gentile neighbors because they refused to participate in emperor worship. These tensions led to the eruption of the pogrom in Alexandria that we discussed in an earlier lecture. Against this background, the Jews of Alexandria sent a delegation to Rome under the leadership of Philo to appeal to the emperor Gaius.

- At the same time, the emperor ordered the Syrian legate, a man named Petronius, to convert the Jerusalem Temple into a shrine for the cult of the emperor, with a statue of himself, Gaius Caligula, set up in it. Petronius realized that carrying out the emperor's order would be disastrous—the Jews would rebel and riot.

- For this reason, Petronius stalled, pretending he hadn't received the order. Fortunately, in the meantime, Herod Agrippa I had arrived in Rome and heard about the emperor's order. Agrippa intervened with his old friend and convinced Gaius to rescind his order.

Reunification of Herod the Great's Kingdom
- In 37 A.D., Gaius gave Herod Agrippa I the territories of Herod Philip—the very northern territories in the area of the Golan and modern-day Syria. Two years later, Gaius Caligula deposed

Herod Antipas and gave Herod Agrippa I his territories, which included Galilee and Perea.

- A couple of years later, in 41 A.D., Gaius Caligula was assassinated. And at that point, Herod Agrippa I stepped in and played a significant role in successfully convincing the Roman Senate that Claudius should become the next emperor. In return, Claudius confirmed Herod Agrippa I as king and added Judea, Samaria, and Idumea to his kingdom.

- At this point, all the former kingdom of Herod the Great was reunited and ruled by his Hasmonean grandson, Herod Agrippa I. As we might imagine, Herod Agrippa I was fantastically popular among the Jewish population. He had Hasmonean blood flowing in his veins. He had stepped in with Gaius Caligula and prevented the Temple of Jerusalem from being converted into a temple for the worship of the Roman emperor. Herod Agrippa I was widely admired despite the fact that he had been raised in Rome, educated in Rome, and was not himself an observant Jew.

- Christian tradition portrays Herod Agrippa I as a persecutor of the developing church. For example, he had James the son of Zebedee beheaded, and he had Peter arrested. Here is the relevant passage from Acts: "At about that time, King Herod laid violent hands upon some who belonged to the Church. He had John's brother James beheaded. And when he saw that this gratified the Jews, he proceeded to arrest Peter too."

- In the coming decades, Herod's death and the division of his kingdom would lead to the outbreak of the First Jewish Revolt against the Romans, culminating with the destruction of the Second Temple in Jerusalem in the year 70 A.D.

Suggested Reading

Schiffman, *Texts and Traditions*, "Judea under the Procurators," pp. 395–407.

Questions to Consider

1. Who was Herod Antipas, and why did he execute John the Baptist?

2. Who was Herod Agrippa I, and why do later Christian sources portray him as a persecutor of the developing church?

Lecture

19   Anarchy in Judea

Herod Agrippa I, the grandson of Herod the Great, ruled the reunited kingdom of his grandfather until his death at the age of 54 in 44 A.D. At that point, the Roman emperor Claudius made the kingdom part of the Roman province of Syria and placed it under the administration of low-ranking governors, called procurators, who reported to the legate. In this lecture, we discuss these procurators and examine the increasingly anarchic conditions leading up to the outbreak of the First Jewish Revolt against Rome. It was against the background of these events that James the Just, the brother of Jesus, was executed.

Increasing Unrest and Turmoil
- Cuspius Fadus was a procurator who administered the territory of Judea from 44 to 46 A.D. His administration saw the appearance of the messianic figure Theudas, who persuaded followers to accompany him to the Jordan River.
    - Cuspius Fadus sensed danger and attacked the group with his cavalry, which resulted in a bloodbath. Theudas was captured and decapitated, and his head was carried to Jerusalem.

    - The Theudas event is described in Acts 5:35–36: "Men of Jerusalem, take care what you propose to do with these men. For some time ago, Theudas appeared, claiming to be a person of importance, and a group of men numbering some 400 joined him. But he was killed and all his followers were dispersed and disappeared."

- Tiberius Julius Alexander was procurator from 46 to 48 A.D. Although Tiberius Julius Alexander was the nephew of Philo of Alexandria, he repudiated his Jewish faith. Later, during the First Jewish Revolt, Tiberius Julius Alexander became a traitor, advising the Roman commander during the siege of Jerusalem.

- Ventidius Cumanus served as procurator from 48 to 52 A.D. During his administration, the unrest in the country continued. The first incident occurred at Passover, one of the major pilgrimage holidays to the Temple of Jerusalem. A Roman soldier made an indecent gesture to the Jews, which incited the crowd of thousands of pilgrims. When they began to throw stones at the Roman soldiers, Cumanus called for reinforcements. Flavius Josephus notes, "20,000 to 30,000 Jews were killed in the stampede that followed."

- Antonius Felix administered the area from 52 to 60 A.D. He was known in Roman circles for his three marriages, all of them to members of royal families. In fact, one of his wives was the granddaughter of Mark Antony and Cleopatra. But interestingly, another one of his wives was Drusilla, the daughter of Herod Agrippa I and the sister of Herod Agrippa II. In other words, she was a Hasmonean princess.

- When Herod Agrippa I died, Claudius decided not to give Herod Agrippa II the kingdom of his father. But he did bestow on Herod Agrippa II the old territories ruled by Herod Philip in the north, as well as a small kingdom in Lebanon called Chalcis. Furthermore, Claudius gave Herod Agrippa II oversight of the Temple of Jerusalem and the right to appoint high priests.

- When Nero became Roman emperor in 54 A.D., he reconfirmed Antonius Felix as procurator and gave Herod Agrippa II additional territories to rule in the north. These territories were overwhelmingly Gentile.

Emergence of Terrorists and Messiahs

- As each procurator succeeded another, conditions grew increasingly anarchic in Judea, with frequent tensions between the populations of the local districts. This period also saw the appearance of a Jewish urban terrorist group, called the Sicarii, whose name comes from the Latin word *sica*, meaning "dagger."

- Josephus describes the Sicarii: "There's springing up another sort of robber in Jerusalem called Sicarii, who slew men in the daytime in the midst of the city. This they did chiefly at festivals when they mingled among the multitude and concealed daggers under their garments with which they stabbed those who were their enemies. When any fell down dead, the murderer joined in the cries of indignation."

- In addition to terrorist groups, messianic and prophetic figures emerged. Josephus describes an Egyptian Jew who claimed that he would destroy the walls of Jerusalem with a command while standing on the Mount of Olives. This happened during the administration of Antonius Felix. Felix killed or captured hundreds of the messiah's followers, but the Egyptian Jew escaped.

- There was also class warfare at this time, even among various levels of the priesthood. A famous passage from rabbinic literature says, "Woe is me because of the house of Ishmael, son of Phabi [a high priest family]—woe is me because of their fists."

Paul's Arrest and Execution

- It was during this time of political and social turmoil that Paul was arrested. According to Acts 21, Paul was seized by "Jews from Asia" as he exited the Temple:

    They seized him, shouting, "Fellow Israelites, help! This is the man who is teaching

Although Acts tells us that Paul purified himself before entering the Temple, he was arrested on suspicion of bringing a Gentile into the Temple building itself.

everyone everywhere against our people, our law, and this place. More than that, he has actually brought Greeks into the temple and has defiled this holy place." ... They seized Paul and dragged him out of the temple, and immediately the doors were shut. While they were trying to kill him, word came to the tribune of the cohort that all of Jerusalem was in an uproar.

- There are several interesting aspects about this passage. Paul was arrested on suspicion of having brought a non-Jew, a Gentile, into the area of the Temple of Jerusalem—the part that was forbidden to non-Jews. The name of the Gentile was Trophimus of Ephesus, a Greek name.

- Those sounding the alarm were Jews from Asia Minor, the area of modern Turkey. Of course, Paul was from Tarsus, which is in Asia Minor. The Jews recognized both Paul and Trophimus of Ephesus. When the alarm was sounded, the Romans intervened. They sent troops and took Paul into protective custody. Nearly 500 troops then escorted Paul to Caesarea, where he was imprisoned for nearly two years.

- Porcius Festus served as procurator of Judea from 60 to 62 A.D. When he took office, he found the country overrun by gangs and Paul languishing in prison. Porcius Festus sent Paul to Rome, where he was probably executed in 62 A.D.
    - In the ancient world, the manner of execution varied depending not only on the crime but also on the social status of the accused. Paul, of course, claimed to be a Roman citizen; as such, he would have been entitled to a trial in Rome, which is why the local Roman procurator at first did not know what to do with Paul. Verification of Paul's claim of citizenship would have been required; once it was verified, Paul would have been shipped back to Rome for trial. Then, presumably after the trial, he was executed.

○ This is in contrast, of course, to what happened to Jesus. Jesus was not a Roman citizen; he was a lower-class Jew from Galilee. He was executed by the local prefect, Pontius Pilate, using crucifixion, a method that the Romans used for the lower classes, slaves, and common criminals because it was a prolonged and painful way to die.

The Execution of James the Just

- Porcius Festus died in office in 62 A.D., and there was an interval of several months when there was no local Roman procurator. This set up a situation whereby the high priest in Jerusalem, Hanan, took the opportunity to convene the Sanhedrin, the Jewish law court. He brought James the Just, the brother of Jesus, before the Sanhedrin on a charge of breaking Jewish law.

- We are not concerned here with whether James the Just was related to Jesus by blood as a full brother or half-brother or was not related to Jesus by blood at all. He was the leader of the early Christian community in Jerusalem. The term "early Christian community" is highly anachronistic, however; this was still very much a Jewish sect.

- In fact, James the Just was so called because he was known as a pious and law-abiding Jew. He also lived an ascetic lifestyle, as the leader of a community that lived in communal poverty.

- Following is Josephus's description of the trial and execution of James the Just by the Sanhedrin: "So he [Hanan] assembled the Sanhedrin of the judges and brought before them the brother of Jesus who was called Christ, whose name was James, and some others. And when he had formed an accusation against them as breakers of the law, he delivered them to be stoned."

- James was executed by the Sanhedrin on a charge of violating Jewish law. It had to be a false charge, however, because James was known as a law-abiding Jew. His execution most likely reflects the hostility of the elite toward James and his group.

James was known to preach against the accumulation of wealth and the lifestyle of the elites.

- Notice that the circumstances surrounding the death of Jesus and that of James are quite different. Jesus was executed for treason by the Romans, using the means of crucifixion. James was sentenced to death by stoning. Sources suggest that Jewish law courts never used crucifixion as a method of execution.

- Interestingly, James's execution aroused the opposition of moderate Jews and the Pharisees, who brought charges against Hanan to Herod Agrippa II. Hanan was subsequently removed from his post as high priest.

- The intriguing aspect of this episode is that although we see divisions between the various Jewish sects and tensions between them—specifically between the high priest and the Jerusalem elite, on the one hand, and James and his movement, on the other hand—we see some of these groups occasionally aligning with each other against a common enemy.

Suggested Reading
Magness, *The Archaeology of the Holy Land*, chapter 9, "The Early Roman Period."

Questions to Consider
1. What events led to Paul's arrest, as described in the Book of Acts?

2. Why was James the Just arrested and executed?

Lecture

20   Jesus's Prophecy: Jerusalem's Destruction

In this lecture, we survey the many battles associated with the First Jewish Revolt against Rome, which culminated disastrously with the fall of Jerusalem and the destruction of the Second Temple in 70 A.D. We review the passages in the Gospels that record Jesus's foretelling of the destruction of the Temple of Jerusalem and conclude by examining other traditions in the Gospel accounts, aside from Jesus's famous prophecy, that allude to this pivotal event in the history of Judaism and early Christianity.

Hostilities between Gentiles and Jews
- The First Jewish Revolt against Rome began in 66 A.D., when hostilities erupted between Jews and Gentiles in Caesarea and Jerusalem. Herod Agrippa II tried to intervene, without success.

- Josephus describes Herod Agrippa II's attempt to stop the situation from deteriorating any further: "Later, he, Herod Agrippa II, attempted to persuade the multitude to obey Florus [the local governor] until Caesar would send someone to succeed him. But they were, thereby, more provoked, cast reproaches upon the King and had him excluded from the city. Indeed, some of the rebellious had the impudence to throw stones at him."

- At this point, Herod Agrippa II dispatched 2,000 of his own troops to Jerusalem and attempted to drive out the insurgents. But after a week of fighting, the rebels managed to take the Temple of Jerusalem as well as the Upper City, where the Hasmonean Palace was located.

- The rebels burned down the house of the high priest and the public archives. They captured Antonia Fortress, a strategic stronghold overlooking the Temple Mount; massacred the Roman troops protecting Herod's palace; and burned the palace.

- Herod Agrippa II had been unable to protect the city, and the Roman governor was too low-ranking to command a legion. It fell to the legate in Syria, who was based in Antioch, to try to come in and restore order. The legate, Cestius Gallus, entered the field sometime in September of 66 A.D.

- Cestius Gallus headed south from Antioch with four legions—each with approximately 5,000 soldiers—plus another 15,000 troops that had been supplied by Herod Agrippa II. The Roman forces moved south along the coast, taking Jaffa along the way, as well as Sepphoris and Galilee. When Cestius Gallus arrived in Jerusalem, he set up camp on top of Mount Scopus, a northern peak of the Mount of Olives.

- From this strategic position, he launched an assault but met with stiff resistance. As the Roman army withdrew, the retreat turned into a rout. In Josephus's description, the Jewish rebels "plundered the corpses, collected the booty, which had been left on the route, and with songs of triumph retraced their steps to the capital."

- From the Romans' point of view, this decisive defeat was not only unexpected but also deeply humiliating. What's more, it was a turning point. From that moment on, it was clear that all-out war was inevitable.

Progress of the Revolt

- At this point, those who were strongly pro-Roman left the city of Jerusalem. Many moderate Jews, however, chose to stay. The initial provisional government, set up by the rebels, had the moderates in control. The government divided the country into seven districts and put a general in charge of each district. Flavius Josephus was put in charge of the Galilee district.

- We know from Josephus's writings that he had many problems administering Galilee, because of the radical rebel leaders who opposed him. His bitterest enemy was a rebel leader named

John son of Levi of Gischala, or Gush Halav. Another rebel leader was Simon bar Giora, who came from the district of Perea, the area on the east side of the Jordan River and the Dead Sea.

> From his bases at Caesarea Maritima and Scythopolis, Vespasian launched attacks against towns and fortresses in the area of Galilee.

- Of course, the Romans would not accept defeat. After the downfall of Cestius Gallus, Emperor Nero appointed another general to put down the revolt: Vespasian. In the spring of 67 A.D., he arrived in Antioch, which was the base of operation for the Romans. Vespasian assembled 60,000 Roman troops, accompanied by auxiliary troops and other forces, and marched south.

- Once Vespasian reached the country, he established military bases at Caesarea Maritima, to the west on the coast, and at Scythopolis or Beit She'an, located to the east in the Jordan River Valley.

- Vespasian then marched against various towns and strongholds in the area of Galilee. One of these was a town called Jotapata (in Hebrew, Yodfat), where the Romans conducted a siege for 47 days. It was at Yodfat that Josephus himself was taken into custody by Vespasian.

- Another battle occurred at the town of Magdala, on the northwest shore of the Sea of Galilee. This town is noted as the hometown of Mary Magdalene. At Magdala, a Roman flotilla chased rebels who were attempting to escape across the Sea of Galilee and massacred them. Josephus describes this particular event as being so bloody that the water in the Sea of Galilee actually turned red.

- Another important battle took place at a town called Gamla, which is located in the Golan just overlooking the Sea of Galilee from the east. The Romans actually set up a siege wall around the city and used heavy artillery to break through the fortification walls of the town. They managed to break into the town but were repelled, capturing Gamla only after heavy fighting and many losses.

- Vespasian then set up winter camp to wait until spring arrived. His strategy was to isolate Jerusalem before besieging it. In the spring of 68 A.D., Vespasian marched against Perea and took Jericho and Qumran. At this point, it should have been easy to get the rest of the country subdued and take Jerusalem, but that did not happen.

- Events in Rome delayed the continuation of Vespasian's campaign: Emperor Nero had committed suicide. With Nero dead, Vespasian had to wait for fresh orders from a new emperor. But those orders didn't come because the situation in Rome deteriorated over the course of the next year. In fact, 69 A.D. was called in Roman history the Year of the Four Emperors, when there was a rapid succession of men on the throne.

- While Vespasian was waiting for his orders, refugees were pouring into Jerusalem. Specifically, sources tell us that three different rebel factions had divided up and occupied different parts of the city. These factions were led by Simon bar Giora, John of Gischala, and Eleazar.

Destruction of the Second Temple
- In 69 A.D., Vespasian's troops proclaimed him emperor of the Roman Empire. While Vespasian went to Rome to take over as emperor, he left his son Titus in charge of besieging Jerusalem. Before attacking the city, however, Titus attempted to get the Jews to surrender; but his terms of surrender were rejected.

- Thus, the Romans launched their attack against the city. They were able to breach the area of the Temple Mount by taking the Antonia Fortress. Interestingly, Josephus reports that on that day, the daily sacrifices in the Temple of Jerusalem ceased, probably for lack of lambs. Josephus notes that at the point when the sacrifices ceased, the presence of the God of Israel departed from Jerusalem and the Second Temple.

- Fighting now spread onto the Temple Mount. Titus attacked the Second Temple, and in the fighting, the Temple was set on fire. According to Josephus, the destruction of the Temple by fire was not intentional on Titus's part. Josephus reports that a soldier "snatched a brand from the burning timber and, hoisted up by one of his comrades, flung the fiery missile through a low golden door, which gave access on the north side to the chambers surrounding the sanctuary."

- Titus and his commanders entered the burning Temple of Jerusalem and the Holy of Holies, removing some of its contents. Although the Second Temple had been destroyed, this was not the end of the revolt. Parts of the city still held out against the Romans—specifically the Upper City, the area of the elite residences and the palaces. The battle in the Upper City continued for another month, into September, with the rebel leaders making their last stand in Herod's palace before they were captured.

Judea as an Independent Roman Province

- With the fall of Jerusalem and the destruction of the Second Temple, Vespasian and Titus staged a victory parade, in which the booty and the prisoners were marched along the victory route through Rome. Among the prisoners paraded through Rome were John of Gischala and Simon bar Giora. At the Temple of Capitoline Jupiter, the procession was halted. Simon was taken to be scourged and executed, and John was sentenced to life in prison.

- Emperor Vespasian then built a temple dedicated to peace in the Roman Forum to house and display the spoils from the Temple of Jerusalem, including the famed seven-branched candelabrum.

- After the revolt, the Romans made Judea an independent Roman province. This meant that Judea now had its own legion permanently stationed in Jerusalem under the command of a legate.

Gospel Allusions to the Fall of Jerusalem

- We have previously discussed Jesus's well-known prophecy regarding the destruction of the Second Temple. But there are also other passages in the Gospel accounts that might allude to the fall of Jerusalem. Two examples come from Matthew.

- In the Parable of the Wicked Tenants, Matthew talks about the tenants of an absentee landlord, who killed the slaves and the landlord's son: "Now, when the owner of the vineyard comes, what will he do to those tenants? They said to him, he will put those wretches to a miserable death and release the vineyard to other tenants who will give him the produce at the harvest time." The parable reflects the biblically rooted idea of the God of Israel as the owner of the vineyard and Jews as the tenants.

- Another parable in Matthew that might allude to the destruction of Jerusalem and the Second Temple is the Parable of the Wedding Banquet. In this story, a king sent his slaves to invite guests to a wedding banquet for his sons. But the intended guests refused to come and killed the slaves. Matthew says that the king was outraged and sent his troops to destroy the murderers and burn their city. Of course, the burning of the city here recalls the burning of the city of Jerusalem by the Romans in 70 A.D.

Suggested Reading

Goldenberg, *The Origins of Judaism*, chapter 7, "A Century of Disasters."

VanderKam, *An Introduction to Early Judaism*, "The Roman Period," pp. 32–52.

Questions to Consider

1. Why was the defeat of Cestius Gallus a turning point in the outbreak of the First Jewish Revolt?

2. How did Vespasian and Titus celebrate their victories over the Jews?

Lecture 21
Flavius Josephus: Witness to 1st Century A.D.

Flavius Josephus is perhaps our best-known ancient Jewish author. He provides much of our information about the history of the Jews and Judaism in the Second Temple period. Because of Josephus's account of the First Jewish Revolt, we are better informed about this conflict than about any other native rebellion against Rome. Ironically, however, Josephus's writings were preserved by Christians rather than Jews. In this lecture, we survey the life and writings of Flavius Josephus and conclude by considering Josephus's significance in later Jewish and Christian traditions.

Flavius Josephus
- Flavius Josephus is the major source of information we have drawn on throughout all the lectures in this course. His writings were preserved by Christians because he was a witness to the time of Jesus and the period after the death of Jesus. We cannot talk about Jesus and his Jewish influences without the work of Flavius Josephus.

- Josephus was a Jew—a Judean—named Joseph son of Matthias (in Hebrew, Yosef ben Matityahu). But we know him better by his Roman name, Flavius Josephus. He was born in Judea in 37 A.D., the year Gaius Caligula became emperor; he died in Rome shortly after 100 A.D.

- Josephus was from an aristocratic, priestly family and had Hasmonean blood on his mother's side. Our biographical information about Josephus comes from his own writings about himself, including an autobiography.

- Josephus tells us that when he was a young man, he was precocious and curious. At the age of 16, he set out to learn firsthand about the three major sects of Judaism—the Pharisees, Sadducees, and Essenes—by spending time with each one of them. In fact, Josephus is our only outside ancient author who claims to have firsthand knowledge of the Essenes. Josephus chose to become a Pharisee.

Commander of Galilee
- In 67 A.D., after the First Jewish Revolt against the Romans broke out and the Jews formed a provisional government, Josephus was appointed commander of Galilee. This is the part of the country that was first attacked by Vespasian and his forces as they moved south from Antioch. There were a series of battles throughout Galilee, with the Romans taking various cities and strongholds; the last fortress, which remained under Josephus's command, was Jotapata, or Yodfat.

- There, Josephus and his forces were under siege for 47 days before the fortress was taken by the Romans. According to Josephus, after he surrendered at Jotapata, he was taken alive to Vespasian, the Roman general. Vespasian did not kill Josephus because Josephus predicted that one day Vespasian would become emperor of the Roman Empire.

- Of course, in 69 A.D., a year after Nero died, Vespasian did become emperor. At that point, Vespasian set Josephus free. Subsequently, Josephus Latinized his name to Flavius Josephus, adopting Vespasian's family name. (Vespasian founded the Flavian dynasty.) Josephus then became a client of the imperial family.

The Jewish War and *Jewish Antiquities*
- After the fall of Jerusalem, Josephus settled in Rome. He received Roman citizenship and was commissioned by his patrons, the Flavian family, to write a series of history books about the Jewish people. With his Roman imperial patrons looking over his shoulder, Josephus wrote an account called *The Jewish War*, which was completed sometime around 80 A.D.

- Interestingly, Josephus doesn't begin *The Jewish War* with the outbreak of the First Jewish Revolt against the Romans; he starts long before that, with a discussion of the sequence of events that led to the establishment of the Hasmonean dynasty. Because *The Jewish War* seeks to trace the reasons for the outbreak of the revolt, it goes back to the time of the Maccabees and the Hasmoneans.

- It is not a coincidence that Josephus sets up his account of the First Jewish Revolt in this way. He was influenced by Greek histories and historians, and his account of the First Jewish Revolt was consciously modeled after such Greek histories as Thucydides's *History of the Peloponnesian War*, by seeking to trace the origins of the conflict back to its beginning.

- About a decade later, around 93 or 94 A.D., Josephus finished his second major work, called *Jewish Antiquities* or *Antiquities of the Jews*. This was a much more ambitious project than *The Jewish War* because it was intended to present the entire scope of Jewish history to a Roman audience. *Antiquities* begins with the biblical account of creation and ends on the eve of the outbreak of the First Jewish Revolt.

- Because some of the events in both works overlap, we actually have two different accounts in Josephus of many of the same historical events. Indeed, the tone of these two large works is quite different. *Antiquities* was written at a time when the revolt against the Romans was less immediate; it seeks to exalt the Jewish people in the eyes of the Greco-Roman world. By the time Josephus wrote *Antiquities*, he had been living as a Diaspora Jew in Rome for a couple of decades—a situation that influenced his outlook.

Nonobjective Historical Accounts
- It is crucial to remember that the writings of Josephus are not objective historical works in the modern sense of the word. They must be used with caution, because Josephus clearly

was motivated by political considerations, self-justification, and apologetic tendencies.

- For example, it is evident that Josephus did not want his readers to know that the revolt was supported by some members of the Jewish aristocracy; instead, he gave the impression that it was the work of a few fanatics. In fact, when the Jews first set up their provisional government, it was led by moderates, not fanatics.

- Josephus's apologetic for the Romans is equally apparent. Vespasian and Titus are portrayed as leaders who gave the Jews every opportunity to come to their senses and surrender. For example, as we saw, Josephus tells us that Titus was not at fault for the burning of the Second Temple; according to Josephus, Titus even wept when he saw the destruction.

- Compare Josephus's account with a contemporary description of the destruction of the Second Temple in a Roman source, that of the Roman historian Tacitus. According to Tacitus, Titus actually ordered the Temple's destruction—exactly contrary to what Josephus describes.

- Josephus chose to end his massive seven-volume work, *The Jewish War*, with the mass suicide of the Jewish rebels at Masada. Because Josephus is our only ancient source for this event, in recent years, scholars have questioned whether the mass suicide actually took place.

Flavian Propaganda

- *The Jewish War* also served, in part, as propaganda for the newly established Flavian dynasty, which legitimized itself on the basis of the Roman victory over the Jews. The Flavians needed to establish their legitimacy, because they were not connected in any familial way to the previous dynasty.

- The Flavians used their victory over the Jews as a means of legitimizing themselves. They broadcast their victory in every

The Colosseum—the Flavian Amphitheatre—was built with money brought by the spoils of the First Jewish Revolt.

way possible, including using the spoils of the war to fund the construction of public monuments around Rome. For example, the Flavians built the monumental Arch of Titus, straddling the Sacred Way in the Roman Forum.

- In addition, the Flavians publicized their victory over the Jews by minting a special series of coins called Judaea Capta ("Judea has been conquered") coins. Interestingly, this is the first time that Roman generals celebrated a victory over a people who were already under Roman rule.

Josephus in the Christian Tradition
- Flavius Josephus's writings are well preserved because of the Christians, who were interested in his chronicle of the time of Jesus and the events after the death of Jesus, leading up to the destruction of the Second Temple in Jerusalem.

- For example, *Antiquities* includes a passage in which Josephus refers to Jesus Christ. This passage, however, is somewhat controversial among scholars. We are not sure whether Josephus actually originally referred to Jesus Christ or whether later Christians who copied Josephus's works inserted the reference to Jesus. Similarly, there are passages in Josephus that concern John the Baptist, and there is a passage concerning the trial and execution of James the Just.

- One reason that Josephus's works were not preserved in the Jewish tradition is that the later rabbis—the sages after 70 A.D.—viewed the Jewish rebels at the time of the First Jewish Revolt as crazed fanatics who brought disaster on Israel.

- Further, the rabbis were not interested in preserving writings that were not sacred scripture or not part of the rabbinic tradition of oral law. Josephus's historical writings were of no interest to them. Most of the Jewish literary works that we have from the centuries after the destruction of the Second Temple are rabbinic writings.

Jesus's Prophecy
- The social tensions and eschatological expectations that impelled Judea to war with Rome were not uniquely Jewish. These tensions were endemic to ancient societies and often contributed to native rebellions. Like the Jews, other rebels in antiquity dreamed of overcoming the Roman Empire.

- What made the First Jewish Revolt against the Romans so special was its intensity, its duration, and the fact that an ancient historian wrote about it in great detail.

- Finally, and perhaps most important for us, the First Jewish Revolt against Rome has retained a significance far beyond the Jewish tradition because Jesus is said to have foreseen the destruction of the Second Temple. According to Matthew 24:1–2, "Jesus left the temple and was going away when his disciples came up to him to call attention to the temple buildings. But he answered, 'Do you not see all this? I tell you not one stone will be left here upon another, but shall be torn down.'"

Suggested Reading

Magness, *The Archaeology of the Holy Land*, chapter 10, "The Early Roman Period."

Schiffman, *Texts and Traditions*, chapter 9, "Revolt and Restoration," pp. 429–469.

Questions to Consider

1. What are some of Josephus's biases and apologetics?

2. Why were Josephus's writings preserved by Christians but not Jews?

Lecture

22 Rabbinic Judaism's Traditions about Jesus

In this lecture, we discuss the impact that the fall of Jerusalem and the destruction of the Second Temple had on Judaism in the decades and centuries afterward. We review the events surrounding the Second Jewish Revolt, or the Bar Kokhba Revolt, between 132 and 135 A.D., which led to extremely punitive measures against the Jews by the emperor Hadrian. We conclude by examining the rise of Rabbinic Judaism—the transformation of Judaism from a sacrificial cult, led by a priesthood, to a community-based religion centered on prayer and worship in synagogues.

Apocalyptic Works

- In the aftermath of the fall of Jerusalem and the destruction of the Second Temple, a number of apocalyptic works were composed. The intention was to reassure readers that, in fact, the violence was all part of God's plan and that the righteous would be delivered through the Messiah. These apocalyptic works include 4 Ezra, 2 Baruch, and the Book of Revelation, or the Apocalypse of John, in the New Testament.

- The works 4 Ezra and 2 Baruch are Pseudepigrapha, which means that they are attributed to people other than their authors. The book 4 Ezra presents Ezra as a lawgiver like Moses, as well as the recipient of heavenly mysteries through divine revelation.

- In the following passage, notice the concern with the revelation of divine secrets by God through an intermediary figure: "And it came to pass on the third day, while I was sitting under an oak, behold a voice came out of a bush opposite me and said, Ezra, Ezra. And I said, here I am, Lord. And I rose to my feet. Then he said to me, I revealed myself in a bush and spoke to Moses. And I led him up to Mount Sinai. And I kept him with me many days and showed him the secrets of the times and declared to him the end of the times."

Aftermath of the First Jewish Revolt

- In the aftermath of the First Jewish Revolt against the Romans and the destruction of the Second Temple, the Romans made major administrative changes in Judea; these were intended to remedy weaknesses in their earlier governing policies.

- The province of Judea was now made independent of Syria, and it was placed under the administration of an imperial senatorial legate—a legate who commanded a legion. Now, a legion was permanently stationed in Jerusalem.

- After 70 A.D., Jerusalem lay in ruins for a number of years. What's more, the sects of the late Second Temple period—Pharisees, Sadducees, and Essenes—disappeared from the historical record.

The Diaspora Revolt

- Jews in the decades after 70 A.D. lived in daily anticipation of the reestablishment of the Temple of Jerusalem. But of course, the Jews would have needed permission from the Romans to rebuild the Temple. As the years went by and Roman permission was not forthcoming, the Jews began to grow increasingly anxious.

- Eventually, this anxiety and unmet expectations erupted in a series of revolts against the Romans. The first of these revolts is called the Diaspora Revolt (115–117 A.D.), which broke out among Jews living in Diaspora communities. It began in Egypt, then spread to other Diaspora groups.

- Although we have almost no sources of information about this revolt, all indications are that it was brutally suppressed by Emperor Trajan. What we do know is that this revolt was apparently fueled by messianic expectations and reflected pent-up hostilities between Jews and non-Jews.

The Second Jewish Revolt

- Several decades later, another revolt broke out, known as the Second Jewish Revolt, or the Bar Kokhba Revolt, after its leader.

The Bar Kokhba Revolt (132–135 A.D.) was instigated following a trip to the eastern provinces by Trajan's successor, Hadrian.

- In 129–130 A.D., Emperor Hadrian toured the eastern provinces of the Roman Empire. During the course of this tour, he visited Jerusalem. When Hadrian saw the city still lying in ruins, he decided to rebuild it—not as a Jewish city but as a Roman one.
  - In fact, following the precedent set by Alexander the Great, Hadrian decided to name the rebuilt city in honor of himself. He called it Aelia Capitolina.

  - *Aelia* was Hadrian's middle name, and *Capitolina* reflects the fact that the new patron deity of this Roman city would not be the God of Israel but the chief deity of the Roman pantheon, Capitoline Jupiter. Hadrian's plans were to dedicate a new temple on the Temple Mount to Capitoline Jupiter.

- Imagine the impact that this decision had on the Jews, who had been living in daily expectation of the rebuilding of the Temple of Jerusalem. Not surprisingly, after Hadrian departed, the Jews rose up against the Romans, led by a messianic figure named Simon ben Kosiba.

- In this second revolt, it became evident that the Jews had learned their lessons from the First Jewish Revolt. Instead of trying to fight the Romans on their own terms, the Jewish rebels conducted a campaign of guerrilla warfare. This strategy was very effective. In fact, during the course of the revolt, the Jewish rebels managed to wipe out an entire Roman legion. Hadrian ended up sending one-third of the entire Roman army to Judea to put down the revolt.

- Eventually, however, the tide turned against the Jews. The last fortress to fall to the Romans was Betar, which was located near Bethlehem. According to sources, this is where Bar Kokhba himself was killed. Betar fell on the ninth day of the month of Av (August), which in Jewish tradition is a day that commemorates the destruction of both the First and the Second Temples. That day, therefore, is more a theological symbol than an actual historical date.

Punitive Measures against the Jews
- The Bar Kokhba Revolt had significant and long-lasting consequences for Jews and Judaism. Following it, Hadrian instituted a number of punitive measures against the Jews and Judaism. Most of the Jewish settlements in Judea were destroyed, and the Jewish population was killed or dispersed. Many Jews were now concentrated in the northern part of the country, in the area of Galilee and the Golan.

- Hadrian also went ahead with his plans to rebuild Jerusalem, which now became a Roman colony. What's more, Hadrian prohibited Jews from living in the city of Jerusalem and its environs. Hadrian did something else that was new in the Roman world: He issued an edict restricting the practice of Judaism, including prohibiting circumcision.

- Until this time, Judaism had been a legal religion in the Roman Empire, with Jews free to worship the God of Israel and live according to God's laws. Hadrian also changed the name of the province from Judea to Syria Palaestina. *Palaestina* was a revival of the term *Philistia*, referring to the kingdom of the Philistines.

Rabbinic Judaism
- The Bar Kokhba Revolt put an end to Jewish hopes that the Temple of Jerusalem would be rebuilt any time soon. By all accounts, Judaism should have disappeared at this point, because the religion was based on a sacrificial cult centered on the Temple of Jerusalem.

- However, Judaism survived by transforming itself from a sacrificial cult, led by a priesthood and centered on a temple structure, to the kind of religion it is today—a community-based religion centered on prayer and worship in synagogues. This transformation occurred after the Bar Kokhba Revolt in an era known as the period of Rabbinic Judaism; the transformation came about largely under the leadership of a group of men called rabbis.

- In ancient times, rabbis were men who were schooled in the Torah. The origins of the rabbis of Rabbinic Judaism are unclear, however. Many scholars believe that the Pharisees of the late Second Temple period were the dominant element in this new group. One of the reasons for this speculation is that rabbinic interpretations of Jewish law often resemble teachings of the Pharisees.

- The rabbis and their students occupied themselves with studying and interpreting the Torah—written law—as well as the tradition of oral law. In about 200 A.D., Rabbi Judah ha-Nasi compiled and edited this corpus of oral law into a collection called the Mishnah, which means the "Teaching." The Mishnah was divided into six parts, according to topic or theme:
  - *Zeraim* ("Seeds"): agricultural laws

  - *Moed* ("Appointed Times"): laws dealing with the Sabbath and festivals

  - *Nashim* ("Women"): marriage and divorce regulations

  - *Nezikin* ("Damages"): civil and criminal laws

  - *Kodashim* ("Holy Things"): laws dealing with the Temple of Jerusalem and sacrifices

  - *Tohorot* ("Purification"): laws dealing with Jewish ritual purity.

- Eventually, a commentary on the Mishnah was compiled, called the Gemara, or "Completion." Together, the Mishnah and the Gemara are called the Talmud. Today, the Talmud still serves as the authoritative basis for Jewish religious life.

In one passage of rabbinic literature, Jesus's name is invoked to save the life of a boy, but because of that invocation, the boy's life is lost in the world to come.

Jesus in the Rabbinic Tradition
- When we examine the writings of the Christian church fathers, we see many references to Jews and Judaism, including attacks against them. Both religious traditions laid claim to a shared heritage. Interestingly, though, rabbinic literature does not contain many direct references to Christianity.

- There are, however, a few passages in rabbinic literature that refer to Jesus. Of course, he is not called Jesus Christ; sometimes he is called Jesus the Nazarene or Jesus of Nazareth: Yeshu ha-Notzri. He is also known as Jesus, son of Pandera (or Pantera). This name refers to Jesus as the illegitimate son of Miriam and a Roman, or non-Jewish, soldier named Pantera.

- The rabbinic traditions frequently portray Jesus as an illegitimate child, and some talk about Jesus either as a magician or in connection with magical practices. In one specific passage, Jesus's name is invoked for its power to save a boy from choking. The point of the passage, however, is that although the boy was healed, he lost his life in the world to come, because the name of Jesus had been invoked to heal him.

Suggested Reading
Cohen, *From the Maccabees to the Mishnah*, chapter 7, "The Emergence of Rabbinic Judaism."

Goldenberg, *The Origins of Judaism*, chapter 8, "The Rebirth of Judaism."

Questions to Consider
1. What is the point of such works as 4 Ezra that were written in the aftermath of 70 A.D.?

2. What were the immediate and long-term consequences of the Bar Kokhba Revolt?

Lecture 23 Jesus's Apocalyptic Outlook

Jesus's worldview is widely characterized as apocalyptic and eschatological, meaning that it included an expectation of the imminent arrival of a messiah, the violent overthrow of the current world order, and the establishment of a utopian Kingdom of God. In this lecture, we discuss Jesus's emphasis on moral or ethical behavior within the context of biblical Jewish purity laws and compare his apocalyptic outlook with that of the Qumran sect, which was associated with the Dead Sea Scrolls.

An Apocalyptic Worldview

- Although the notion of Jesus's apocalyptic outlook is not universally accepted by all scholars, the concept clearly has merit. Biblical scholar Bart Ehrman notes, "Jesus stood within a long line of Jewish prophets who understood that god was soon going to intervene in this world, overthrow the forces of evil that ran it, and bring in a new kingdom in which there would be no more war, disease, catastrophe, despair, hatred, sin, or death. And Jesus maintained that this new kingdom was coming soon, that in fact, his own generation would see it."

- In preparation for this new kingdom, Jesus reportedly emphasized the importance of moral and ethical behavior. However, in the Gospel accounts, Jesus is portrayed, above all, as performing miracles—in particular, exorcising demons and healing the sick.

- In fact, Jesus's exorcisms and healings, as well as his emphasis on moral and ethical behavior, should be understood within the context of biblical Jewish purity laws. These laws mandate that only pure and unblemished creatures may be permitted to enter the presence of the God of Israel. Jesus's exorcisms and healings were not merely intended as apocalyptic signs but were performed by Jesus—and his disciples as God's agents—to effect the entry of the diseased and disabled into the eschatological Kingdom of God on earth.

Moral and Physical Impurity

- In contrast, the Qumran sect believed that evil spirits or demons rendered people disabled or diseased, and these evil spirits actually made people impure. Beliefs connecting demons and evil spirits, diseases and disabilities, and impurity and apocalyptic expectations were widespread among the Jewish population during the time of Jesus. Jesus's emphasis on moral or ethical purity reflects his concern to ensure Israel's entry into the Kingdom of God.

Skin diseases, such as leprosy, were considered to be a source of ritual impurity; further, one of the Dead Sea Scrolls indicates that in some Jewish circles, the blind were also considered impure.

- Scholars have observed that Jesus seems to be indifferent to the observance of ritual purity and is far more concerned with emphasizing moral and ethical behavior. The reason may be that ritual impurity is an impermanent condition that can be remedied relatively quickly and easily. As we've seen, reversing ritual impurity is a relatively simple process, usually involving immersion in a pool of water and waiting for a certain amount of time to pass.

- However, certain moral violations—specifically, sexual transgressions, idolatry, and murder—are abominations that defile the land and cause the God of Israel to abandon his sanctuary and his people.

- Moral impurity cannot be cleansed through a process of ritual purification but, instead, requires punishment or atonement. Jesus's repeated exhortations to refrain from immoral or unethical behavior, therefore, reflect a fear of pollution that had the potential to repel God's presence—especially for those who believed that God's kingdom was about to be established on earth.

Beliefs of the Qumran Sect

- Like Jesus, the Qumran sect had an apocalyptic worldview and anticipated the imminent arrival of the eschaton, the end of days. Members of the sect also believed that only pure and unblemished creatures might enter the divine presence. However, in contrast to Jesus, the Qumran sect sought to exclude the blemished and impure.

- The Qumran sect believed that the end of days was imminent and would be marked by the arrival of two—perhaps three— messianic figures, a royal messiah descended from David and a priestly messiah descended from Aaron. These messiahs would play a part in a violent upheaval, a 40-year eschatological war, that would obliterate evil and usher in a utopian era with the establishment of a temple in a new and purified Jerusalem.

- These eschatological expectations of the Qumran sect are described in a Dead Sea Scroll called the Rule of the Congregation. This scroll describes the community in the messianic era. It excludes people who are ritually impure and have various kinds of disabilities and diseases.

- The underlying rationale here is based on biblical Jewish law, according to which only ritually pure and unblemished creatures may enter God's presence, whether it's his tabernacle, the sanctuary, or the eschatological Kingdom of God on earth. Once the Kingdom of God is established on earth, God's presence will dwell on earth, and everyone must be pure and unblemished in that presence.

- The Rule of the Congregation makes it explicit that impure, deformed, and diseased people are excluded from the assembly owing to the presence of the angels of holiness. Conditions of human impurity or physical affliction are precisely those conditions that distinguish humans from angels. The idea is that humans in God's presence should be like angels.

- Other Dead Sea Scrolls provide insight into further eschatological expectations of the Qumran sect. The War Rule not only refers to the royal messiah in connection with the eschatological war but provides a rare glimpse into the utopia expected to follow the war. The Kingdom of God will be established only after there is a violent overthrow of the current world order.

Jesus's Campaign of Exorcisms and Healings
- The Gospel accounts indicate that Jesus shared apocalyptic expectations similar to those of the Qumran sect, including a distinction between a messianic era and a violent upheaval that would usher in the Kingdom of God. Jesus believed that the end of days was already underway with the arrival of a messianic figure, whom Jesus identifies as himself. Exorcising demons, healing the sick, and raising the dead are presented as signs that the Kingdom of God has arrived.

- According to Luke 7:20–22:

  > When the men had come to him they asked, "John the Baptist has sent us to you to ask, are you the one who is to come? Or are we to wait for another?" Jesus had just then cured many people of diseases, plagues, and evil spirits, and had given sight to many who were blind. And he answered them, "Go and tell John that you have seen and heard the blind receive their sight, the lame walk, the lepers are cleansed, the deaf hear, the dead are raised, the poor have good news brought to them."

- Interestingly, Jesus embarked on a campaign of exorcisms and healings immediately after being baptized by John and assembling a group of disciples. According to Mark 1:21, while teaching in the synagogue at Capernaum, Jesus reportedly exorcised a man with an unclean spirit. This was followed by the performance of many more exorcisms and the healing of numerous people who suffered from various diseases and disabilities.

- Also early on, in Mark 1:40–45, we read:

  > A leper came to him begging him, and kneeling, he said to him, "If you choose you can make me clean." Moved with pity, Jesus stretched out his hand and touched him, and said to him, "I do choose. Be made clean." Immediately the leprosy left him and he was made clean. After sternly warning him, he sent him away at once, saying to him, "See that you say nothing to anyone. But go show yourself to the priest and offer for your cleansing what Moses commanded as a testimony to them."

  - What's significant in this passage is the fact that Jesus is cleansing rather than healing the leper, reflecting Jesus's concern with ritual purification. Another interesting aspect of the passage is that Jesus refers the leper to a priest.

- Priests didn't heal lepers. But only priests, according to biblical law, had the authority to diagnose leprosy and pronounce someone cured. Once they did that, the former leper was required to undergo a process of ritual purification. The passage suggests that rather than rejecting ritual purification, Jesus took it for granted.

- According to the Gospel accounts, the afflictions that Jesus cured are leprosy, paralysis, a withered hand, hemorrhages, deafness, dumbness, and blindness. Interestingly, these correspond with the afflictions mentioned in the Rule of the Congregation that disqualify people from admission to the Qumran sect's eschatological assembly.

- Jesus's exorcisms and healings were intended to enable those suffering from diseases, physical deformities, disabilities, unclean spirits, or demonic possession to enter the Kingdom of God. Whereas Jesus's attitude towards the diseased and disabled can be characterized as inclusive and proactive, the Qumran sect's approach was exclusive and reactive. The Qumran sect established strict admission criteria that excluded the diseased and disabled from full membership.

- Jesus's apocalyptic expectations are deeply rooted in biblical Jewish traditions—specifically, that all creatures entering the presence of the God of Israel must be in a state of absolute purity and perfection. In fact, the oracle in Isaiah 35 makes clear the connection between salvation, perfection, and purity:

  > The wilderness and the dry land shall be glad, and the desert shall rejoice and blossom. They shall see the glory of the Lord, the majesty of our God. Then the eyes of the blind shall be opened, and the ears of the deaf unstopped. Then the lame shall leap like deer, and the tongues of the speechless sing for joy. A highway shall be there, and it shall be called the Holy Way. The unclean shall not travel on it,

but it shall be for God's people. No traveler, not even fools, shall go astray.

Suggested Reading
Nickelsburg, *Ancient Judaism and Christian Origins*, "The Eschatological Orientation of Early Christianity," pp. 135–146.

Questions to Consider
1. How do Jesus's apocalyptic outlook and eschatological expectations compare with those of the Qumran sect?

2. How might we understand Jesus's attempts to cure or heal the diseased and disabled in light of his apocalyptic outlook and eschatological expectations?

Lecture

24   Jesus's Teachings and Sayings in Context

This course places Jesus within the context of early Judaism—the Judaism of the late Second Temple period. Studying Jesus's Jewish background provides a better framework for understanding the Gospel accounts about his life and ministry; conversely, the Gospel accounts about Jesus inform our study of Judaism in his time. In this concluding lecture, we consider how selected Gospel passages can be understood within their Jewish context, using passages not considered in previous lectures.

Prohibition against Sexual Transgressions
- A lesser-known episode in the Gospels discusses the origin of the concepts of Gehenna and hell. According to Mark 9:43–48:

    If your hand causes you to stumble, cut it off. It is better for you to enter life maimed than to have two hands and go to Gehenna, to the unquenchable fire. And if your foot causes you to stumble, cut it off. It is better for you to enter life lame than to have two feet and to be thrown into Gehenna. And if your eye causes you to stumble, tear it out. It is better for you to enter the Kingdom of God with one eye than to have two eyes and to be thrown into Gehenna, where their worm never dies and the fire is never quenched.

- If we go back to the biblical Jewish roots of the references to a hand stumbling, the passage specifically refers to male sexual transgressions. Specifically, the Hebrew word *yad* can mean either "hand" or "penis."

- Mark's reference to the foot stumbling likewise refers to sexual transgressions. In biblical Hebrew, the word *regel*, "foot," can be a euphemism for "penis." We see this in Isaiah 6:2, which says, "Seraphs were in attendance above him. Each had six wings.

With two they covered their faces, and with two they covered their feet, and with two they flew."

- Similarly, the stumbling of the eye can refer to male sexual transgressions. The Babylonian Talmud recounts the story of Samson: "Our rabbis have taught Samson rebelled against God through his eyes, as it is said, and Sampson said unto his father, get her for me because she is pleasing in my eyes. Therefore the Philistines put out his eyes, as it is said, and the Philistines laid hold on him and put out his eyes."

Gehenna

- The passage from Mark 9 cited above mentions Gehenna, which to modern readers, connotes hell, but in fact, there is no concept of hell or an afterlife in the Hebrew Bible. Instead, the abode of the dead is called *she'ol*, which means "pit" or "grave." *She'ol* is simply a neutral place of darkness where the dead go.

- In the Septuagint, the ancient Greek translation of the Hebrew Bible, *she'ol* is translated as Hades, which was the Greek underworld or abode of the dead. And interestingly, the New Testament also uses Hades to refer to the underworld. We read in Revelation 1:18, "And I have the keys of death and of Hades."

- Gehenna originally referred to a valley in Jerusalem called the Ben-Hinnom Valley. The Hebrew name, Gai Ben-Hinnom, became Gehenna in Greek. According to the Hebrew Bible, the Ben-Hinnom Valley was the site of idolatry by Israelites and other peoples, including the practice of child sacrifice.

- Mark's phrasing "where their worm never dies and the fire is never quenched" is also rooted in biblical tradition. Specifically, it comes from Isaiah 66:24, which says, "And they shall go out and look at the dead bodies of the people who have rebelled against me. For their worm shall not die, their fire shall not be quenched, and they shall be an abhorrence to all flesh."

Lecture 24—Jesus's Teachings and Sayings in Context | 157

- In the New Testament, death in the eternal fire of Gehenna is juxtaposed against eternal life in the Kingdom of God.

The Temple Tax
- Another episode in the Gospel accounts relates to the temple tax and Jesus's cleansing of the Temple of Jerusalem. In Matthew 17:24–25, we read, "When they reached Capernaum the collector of the temple tax came to Peter and said, 'Does your teacher not pay the temple tax?' He said, 'Yes, he does.'"

- The temple tax was a tax that all adult male Jews were required to pay to the Temple of Jerusalem for the upkeep and maintenance of the sacrificial cult. The temple tax is rooted in biblical law—specifically, in Exodus 30:11–13:

> The Lord spoke to Moses, "When you take a census of the Israelites to register them. At registration all of them shall give a ransom for their lives to the Lord so that no plague may come upon them for being registered. This is what each one who was registered shall give—half a shekel according to the shekel of the sanctuary, half a shekel as an offering to

Jesus's overturning of the tables of the moneychangers in the Temple reflected his opposition to the yearly temple tax and the requirement that it be paid in silver shekels.

the Lord. Each one who is registered from 20 years old and upward shall give the Lord's offering."

- In a related episode, recorded in Matthew 21:12, "Then Jesus entered the temple and drove out all who were selling and buying in the temple, and he overturned the tables of the moneychangers." Modern readers of this passage understand it to mean that Jesus was opposed to commercial activity in the area of the Temple of Jerusalem. However, this is an incorrect and anachronistic understanding of the text.

- In the Matthew passage, the word *temple* refers to the entire Temple Mount, which was a center of commercial activity. It is anachronistic to interpret Jesus's action as opposition to commercial activity on the Temple Mount—this was, in fact, a characteristic feature of all ancient temple complexes.

- The nature of Jesus's objection has to do with the nature of the temple tax and why there were moneychangers actually on top of the Temple Mount. The reason is that the Temple Mount, in addition to being an area of commercial activity, was a place where Jewish pilgrims congregated for the holidays and paid the temple tax.

- Originally, the temple tax as mandated in Exodus was a one-time payment, but under the Hasmoneans, it became an annual tax. Making this an annual tax aroused a great deal of opposition among the Jewish population.

- What's more, the temple tax had to be paid in a certain kind of currency—specifically, in Tyrian tetradrachms, or silver shekels, which contained a high content of silver. Therefore, pilgrims coming to the temple would have to exchange currency to pay the temple tax with this valuable coin.

- What motivated Jesus here was not just an opposition to the annual payment of the temple tax but the fact that this tax had to be paid in a valuable coin that would have been a hardship on the poorer classes—the majority of the Jewish population who were Jesus's supporters.

Jesus as Creator

- The next passage for consideration is Jesus's healing of the blind man, as reported in John 9:1, 6–7: "As he walked along he saw a man blind from birth. When he had said this, he spat on the ground and made mud with the saliva and spread the mud on the man's eyes, saying to him, 'Go wash in the Pool of Siloam.' Then he went and washed, and came back able to see."

- Many modern scholars understand this passage as a reflection of the popular ancient belief in the healing properties of saliva. In a recent article, however, biblical scholar Daniel Frayer-Griggs suggests otherwise. Frayer-Griggs notes that an early church father, Irenaeus, understands Jesus's use of clay to heal the blind man as alluding to God's use of dust in the creation of Adam. In the episode recounted in John, then, Jesus becomes a creator figure.

- The Book of John contains other allusions to the biblical creation story. In John 9:4–5, we read: "We must work the works of him who sent me while it is day, night is coming, when no one can work. As long as I am in the world, I am the light of the world." In John 9:32, Jesus's opponents specifically mention creation: "Never since the world began has it been heard that anyone opened the eyes of a person born blind."

- What's more, John 9:14 emphasizes that the healing took place on the Sabbath, which may reflect the rabbinic notion that God continued the work of creating and sustaining life on the Sabbath: "Now it was the Sabbath day when Jesus made the mud and opened his eyes."

- The substances saliva and mud are the materials of creation. Genesis 2:7 recounts: "Then the Lord God formed man from the dust of the ground and breathed into his nostrils the breath of life, and the man became a living being."

- In fact, Jesus's act of curing blindness in John 9 was not merely an act of healing; it was a work of creation. The Book of John is generally considered to be the latest of the canonical Gospels. And John presents Jesus as more than the Messiah. His Jesus has the power to create—and, therefore, possesses the power of God.

Suggested Reading
Nickelsburg, *Ancient Judaism and Christian Origins*, chapter 7, "Conclusions and Implications."

Questions to Consider
1. What might have motivated Jesus to overturn the tables of the moneychangers in the Temple?

2. How might Jesus's healing of the blind man at the Pool of Siloam as reported by John be understood in light of ancient Near Eastern and Jewish creation traditions?

Bibliography

Cohen, Shaye J. D. *From the Maccabees to the Mishnah*. Philadelphia: Westminster, 1987. An introduction to early Judaism; organized thematically.

Collins, John J. *The Apocalyptic Imagination: An Introduction to Jewish Apocalyptic Literature*. Grand Rapids, MI: Eerdmans, 1998. An overview of Jewish apocalyptic literature.

Ehrman, Bart D. *Jesus, Apocalyptic Prophet of the New Millennium*. Oxford: Oxford University Press, 1999. An overview of Jesus's apocalyptic worldview.

Goldenberg, Robert. *The Origins of Judaism from Canaan to the Rise of Islam*. New York: Cambridge University Press, 2007. A good, succinct textbook covering Israelite religion and early Judaism; arranged chronologically.

Magness, Jodi. *The Archaeology of the Holy Land: From the Destruction of Solomon's Temple to the Muslim Conquest*. New York: Cambridge University Press, 2012. Designed as a textbook for students and nonspecialists; organized chronologically.

———. *The Archaeology of Qumran and the Dead Sea Scrolls*. Grand Rapids, MI: Eerdmans, 2002. An overview of the Dead Sea Scrolls and the archaeological remains at Qumran.

———. *Stone and Dung, Oil and Spit: Jewish Daily Life in the Time of Jesus*. Grand Rapids, MI: Eerdmans, 2011. A discussion of various aspects of Jewish daily life in the time of Jesus.

Maier, John P. *A Marginal Jew: Rethinking the Historical Jesus*. 4 vols. New York: Doubleday, 1991–2009. A massive four-volume study that attempts to reconstruct and understand the historical Jesus.

Nickelsburg, George W. E. *Ancient Judaism and Christian Origins: Diversity, Continuity, and Transformation*. Minneapolis: Fortress Press, 2003. Compares and contrasts fundamental beliefs and practices in early Judaism and Christianity.

———. *Jewish Literature between the Bible and the Mishnah*. Minneapolis: Fortress Press, 2005. A survey of Jewish parabiblical and extrabiblical literature of the Second Temple period.

Richardson, Peter. *Herod, King of the Jews and Friend of the Romans*. Minneapolis: Fortress Press, 1999. An overview of Herod and his reign that is thorough but accessible to nonspecialists.

Saldarini, Anthony. *Pharisees, Scribes and Sadducees in Palestinian Society*. Grand Rapids, MI: Eerdmans, 2001. A classic introduction to the major sects in late Second Temple period Judaism.

Sanders, E. P. *Judaism: Practice and Belief, 63 BCE–66 CE*. Philadelphia: Trinity Press International, 1992. Includes important discussions of Jewish ritual purity practices.

Schiffman, Lawrence H. *Texts and Traditions: A Source Reader for the Study of Second Temple and Rabbinic Judaism*. Hoboken, NJ: Ktav, 1998. Selected readings from ancient primary sources, with brief introductions.

Schürer, Emil. *The History of the Jewish People in the Age of Jesus Christ (175 B.C.–A.D. 135)*. 3 vols. Revised and edited by G. Vermes, F. Millar, M. Goodman, et al. Edinburgh: T & T Clark, 1979–1986. A classic, comprehensive overview of the history of the Jews in the late Second Temple period and up to the Second Jewish Revolt.

VanderKam, James C. *The Dead Sea Scrolls Today*. Grand Rapids, MI: Eerdmans, 1994. A good, succinct introduction to the Dead Sea Scrolls.

———. *An Introduction to Early Judaism*. Grand Rapids, MI: Eerdmans, 2001. A textbook that begins with a chronological overview of early Judaism, followed by thematic sections.

Vermes, Geza. *Jesus the Jew*. Minneapolis: Fortress Press, 1981. A brief but classic study of Jesus in light of his Jewish context.

Image Credits

Page No.

5	© Jupiterimages/liquidlibrary/Thinkstock.
12	© Jorisvo/iStock/Thinkstock.
16	© Joris Van OstaeyeniStock/Thinkstock.
26	© Walt41/iStock/Thinkstock.
32	© sedmak/iStock/Thinkstock.
38	© Jupiterimages/PHOTOS.com/Thinkstock.
42	© iv-serg/iStock/Thinkstock.
56	© Carly Hennigan/iStock/Thinkstock.
61	© PHOTOS.com/Thinkstock.
71	© sedmak/iStock/Thinkstock.
79	© sedmak/iStock/Thinkstock.
81	© flik47/iStock/Thinkstock.
90	© RobertHoetink/iStock/Thinkstock.
99	© ihsanGercelman/iStock/Thinkstock.
103	© Sonysweetlv/iStock/Thinkstock.
111	© Siempreverde22/iStock/Thinkstock.
123	© Jorisvo/iStock/Thinkstock.
129	© plrang/iStock/Thinkstock.
138	© sborisov/iStock/Thinkstock.
146	© sedmak/iStock/Thinkstock.
149	© Steven Wynn/iStock/Thinkstock.
157	© PHOTOS.com/Thinkstock.

Notes

Notes

Notes

Notes